RUBBER ROOSTER MEDIA

HOW TO MAKE TEN MILLION DOLLARS WITH A RUBBER CHICKEN

Amber Garibay is an entrepreneur, writer, photographer, and business owner. She is also a high school dropout and a college dropout. Amber quits most everything that is not right for her. She quit being fat. She quit being broke. She quit being suicidal. She quit being unhealthy, depressed, and abused. Amber teaches wealth building to other quitters in a private Facebook group:

You can join for free.

HOW TO CREATE WEALTH WITH A RUBBER CHICKEN.

Send her an email: rubberroostermedia@gmail.com

Send her a friend request on Facebook: www.facebook.com/asmilelikeyours

Check out her photography business: www.asmilelikeyours.com

Other books by Amber Garibay

THE ADVENTURES OF RUBBER MY YELLOW COCK

JOURNALING AT THE DEVIL'S HOUR: HOW TO TURN $10 INTO $10 MILLION

RUBBER ROOSTER READING RULES

This book is a part of my Ten Million Dollar Plan.

If you want to know what the plan is,

you will need to read every book I write.

My books will be short and easy to read.

My books are for stupid people who want to make money.

Smart people should not read my books.

They already know everything.

Do NOT use the word COCK to identify your rooster.

It offends people who are afraid of rubber chickens.

RUBBER ROOSTER MEDIA BOOKS

An imprint of RUBBER ROOSTER MEDIA AND MARKETING LLC

Grit City Tacoma, Washington

rubberroostermedia.com

First published in the United States of America by KDP

This book is dedicated to my dad.

He made me wise.

He made me tough.

This book is in loving memory of

Pops

He taught me men are from Mars.

And some people hate delicious peaches.

This book is musical.

Each chapter has a soundtrack, much like a movie.

For the best result and reading experience:

Listen to each soundtrack while you read each chapter.

The chapters were written while the songs played.

This first book is raw and unedited.

Nielson Bookscan reported in 2004 that of 1.2 million books tracked, only 25,000 — barely more than 2 percent — sold more than 5,000 copies.

In 2006, Publisher's Weekly said the average book sells less than 500 copies.

I will release a REVISED/EDITED edition

when my story becomes a profitable product.

CONTENTS

When I grow up, I am going to be a famous singer.

If I can't be a famous singer, I will be a famous writer.

Music is every story I have ever written.

Listen to the chapter soundtracks while you read my writing.

You will hear my voice.

BOOK TWO PREVIEW

PART ONE

JUSTIN LOVES JENNY

CHAPTER ONE: DUST IN THE WIND

Chapter Soundtrack: "Dust In The Wind." by Kansas

The guy I am dating will have a real name in my novel after I decide whether he's fact or fiction. Do we have something real and valuable? Or is he a character in a story that will soon end?

"We are just not working out. You need to see it Amber. We can't keep doing this." Justin Hayward thought he had good reason to break up with me. He sat me down to explain, wise to the certainty he'd settled on. He served it as if it were a saucer of warm milk and I were a kitten happy to be lapping. He wanted me to agree with what he was offering. He wanted me to think he had my best interest at heart, that he was doing me some sort of favor, that it was right to call us quits. "You are the only one that refuses to see we are wrong for each other."

I sit across from him in dumb silence. The rage comes quick. I feel it burst from within like a cherry bomb exploded in the middle of me. I am torn apart all at once. My fists fly like shrapnel. I punch him like a man punches another man. With a closed fist and another one coming.

I swear I see the whites of his eyes roll in shock, but then, any satisfaction I glean is only magnified by another blow which lands cleanly on the square of his jaw. I know he feels me after that. I am sure he is afraid of me. He jumps up from the couch to defend himself as I continue my attack. I slug him again. Center body mass. I punch him in his arms. I hit him in his chest. I pound on him like a woman trying to break down the door of a burning house with her children trapped inside. I beat on him like that mama giving chest compressions to limp babies covered in char. They are dead. I am dead. We are dead and the wrath of our passing roars like a poltergeist being fucked by an exorcism.

I know I am hurting him. I am lucky he hasn't started hurting me. Justin Hayward is a formidable man. It's not like him to allow himself to be abused and I am doing all I can to maim him. I see him cringe as he tries to scramble away from my blows. I watch his hands forming fists knowing he could easily lay me out. He must be considering it under the circumstances which are relentless. I'm on him like an angry hornet, stinging with every limb I can hit him with until he tackles me.

I've never known a gentler defense. He throws his body over mine as if he's protecting me instead of saving himself. His hand is on the back of my hair but he's not pulling it. His fingers are spread wide around my skull but he's not crushing it. We fall to the floor, but I never land on it. He absorbs the force of everything as if he was always meant to be the martyr.

"You need to stop this right now or I am calling the police." He threatens me with the only thing that can make things God awful worse. Cops would be criminal. They would have no choice but to take me to jail if they didn't shoot me first. Calling them would be a fatal mistake. I pray he is bluffing but I am not willing to play poker. I go limp like a freshly strangled corpse.

He rolls off of me to stand. I just lay there without moving. Blinking my surrender up at him in Morse code. I am still. He is springing to life. He grabs his phone as if he means to dial. He holds it out at me like it's the holy cross and I am a demon. "Don't you come near me." His voice is too frantic considering. I don't bother getting up. I can't muster a reply. It's over. We're over. There's nothing left to fight for. Not a God damn thing.

Justin is not convinced I am done trying to pulverize him. He retreats from the house. Walking backwards, with both hands and a phone out in front of him as a defensive. I remain motionless, but I am inclined to pop him again as another wave of raw torment twists my soul to savage. *After all that. He's got some nerve.*

His footsteps are heavy on the front porch. They sound like leaving sounds; distant, hollow, permanent. I realize I am never going to see him again, even though I am sure he will be back. His face becomes my memory's muse. I want to remember what he looks like when he's smiling at me, the way his happy eyes crinkle at the corners, a playful grey-blue, warm and soft like a down sweater. I want to be in his arms again, to hear him tell me he's sorry as he kisses my hair, that he didn't mean it, that there's no way he could ever let me go. *How could he?*

It's the questions that make me run after him. I am up and out the door so quick time can't catch me. Justin hasn't gotten very far with his retreating. He's standing in the drive, looking bent, looking injured. He's covered in the red of my anger, with welts raised and puffy. His face is gaunt and sick-like, soured with spoil. I've ruined him. There is no smile when he looks back at me. There is horror. There is wickedness. There is hate. Things are just as I feared they would be. The Justin I knew before is already gone. I stand to face my nemesis.

I put my hands up the same way a bank robber surrenders upon capture. "I am not going to hit you again. I promise. Please just come back inside." I step backwards and into the house as an effort of good faith. He turns to follow, pushing past me as if he doesn't trust the space between us. "Stay away from me. I mean it," he warns as he slides by. His body remains tight. Locked and loaded. Mine is relaxed, slack like a kite without wind until I can barely keep my soul afloat. It's all too heavy, even the air which is pressing down on my lungs as if I should be suffocating instead of breathing.

Dishes come next. Justin takes to washing them like we're normal, like we're good. It's eerie though, the way he's carrying on as if I'm not there anymore. I start to feel like he'd walk right through me if he came near. I'm vanishing in front of him and he doesn't care to miss me. *He will though.* I tell myself as I stand there watching him ignore me. *He's gonna miss me something fierce.* I decide he doesn't realize what he had at the same time I fear he never will.

The clatter of dishes does the talking for us. Pots bang. Glasses clink. Plates break. Or at least that's what I am expecting to see as he slams his hands in and out of the water as if he's trying to drown something underneath the suds. He's red up to his elbows and soapy wet besides. I see his mouth moving as if he's talking to someone, but no sound is coming out of there. Still, everything is so loud he might as well be screaming.

The only thing louder than those dishes is the sound of my own voice. I wasn't expecting to speak but the words are suddenly there, just two of them. They boom like cannons making the whole house shake. "Thank You."

Everything stops after that. Just for a moment. Justin freezes and then shatters. A beast unleashed to bite. "What did you just say?" He's sneering, lip curled, teeth bared.

I see killing in his eyes and for the first time I fear retaliation. He's going to choke the life out of me if I am not careful, *so I am careful.* I don't repeat myself, but it doesn't matter. He repeats the words back to me like they've already stained his brain with insanity. *"Thank You? Did you just Thank Me? You crazy bitch."*

It's not like Justin to cuss at me, but then I've never kicked his ass before. I suppose ass kicking is a crazy bitch thing to do so I don't find offense with his slander. I had it coming and so did he. "You needed your ass kicked." I spit at him with my back curled. He is not the only one with killing eyes. "Thank you for taking it like a man."

I am grateful he did not injure me, even though I feel mortally wounded. For as little as he cared for me, he was at least an admirable ending. I am thankful for that. The rest though. The rest feels like bitterroot stuck up my nose and a throat full of gravel. My mouth is sucking on dust. There's nothing I can say to change things and now I'm choking on words made of splinters.

We stand there then, in the weirdest way. It's as if we are meeting each other for the first time. As strangers, with neither of us wanting to explore a friendship. "It's over Amber. You need to accept it." I hear him tell me what I need to do. There's a breeze playing with my hair and a fly on the wall watching us with an insipid smile. I decide to wait for the dust to settle before allowing the wind to take me.

CHAPTER TWO: THE MORNING AFTER PILL

Chapter Soundtrack: "Somebody That I Used To Know" by Gotye

The morning bleeds on me with sunshine. I retreat like a singed vampire to the dark, pale and hungry. I hear him moving, a floor above me, with me levels below hell. I lay there looking up at the popcorn ceiling remembering a time I took a trip on acid until I am staring at a sky full of maggots crawling all over themselves. The day is so rotten I feel sick. I can feel those ugly bugs crawling around in my guts and I'm sure I'm gonna hurl. I grit my teeth, swallow the bile down, pull the covers back over my head, and quit. I am done with this day before it's even started.

I don't move again until the sound of him becomes a plangent passing but before that I listen to his life begin without me. He opens the back-sliding door to free the dog which is whining like it was beaten by the night before. Paws scratch for traction on linoleum as the dog slides urgently into the kitchen, whimpering and huffing about how it hates being put out on the deck to sleep. "Hey there buddy." Justin sounds chipper as he greets his furry friend. "It's good to see you old man."

"Wharoof." Elvis the dog is still complaining as Justin opens the front door to let him back outside to pee on the lawn, or rather the dirt that could be grass if we ever bothered to plant any. Not long after, the door squeaks back open then slams shut. Elvis is back inside. Justin is thumping his way to the kitchen to make coffee.

My dog Blondie hears the sounds coming from above and jumps down from the bed to join them upstairs. She scratches at the door for me to let her out but I refuse to move. She's not a part of that pack anymore. I glare at her with crimson bloodshot eyes from a small hole I've made under my covers feeling mad that she doesn't know her place. She doesn't belong with them. She's mine. I am taking her with me when I go.

When I go. Where am I going to go? How am I going to go? Dread spreads like gangrene through my soul, slow and toxic. Justin's choice to break up with me means more than the end of our romance. It means he's going to want me out of his house. *His house. None of this is mine. What do I have left?*

I don't realize I am poor until I am forced to think about how little I own. I have a mattress on a box spring frame, enough furniture to decorate my photography studio, which is of course also located in *his house,* I have a nine-thousand-dollar camera (My ability to run my business), and I have talent.

"Nothing is more common than unsuccessful people with talent."

The squeal of faucets being turned tells me Justin has finished his morning coffee and dose of the local news. He's standing in the shower now. I am there with him in my mind. His eyes are closed by water which is rushing past his silvery slate hair but trickling down elsewhere. Elsewhere is hot lazy rivers on flesh. I feel a pang of yearning and lust as I spy on him with my imagination.

My mouth wants to be on his mouth and then linger down, down those trickling rivers of heat. Justin Hayward is hard, lean, and attractive. He is also unassuming and quiet which only adds to my desire. I want him, even now. *It's over Amber. You need to accept it. We are not together anymore.*

Salty tears fall as muddy water from my nose as I am hit in the ribs with a crowbar of pain. I am crippled with agony and need. I need things to be different, but they aren't. *This can't be happening. Please God. I need more time.*

It is happening though. Time is not something I have. My ending arrives like a speeding car slamming into the back of a semi-truck. The impact is so severe it's a wonder there is anything left to see. There are no skid marks, no signs of stopping, almost no proof that the incident even happened. Then I spot bits of bone, with clumps of matted blond hair. There is *blood* dripping from the bumper of the big rig. That is when I know something terrible just took place. Something scary and sinister. Something that kills. I'm cold as I lay there staring at that wreck. My teeth are chattering like bones tap dancing. My eyes are pulled open with lids cut off by scissors. I don't want to look but I have no choice. *There is a body under there. It's crushed inside that tin can.*

The house has gone hollow. I listen for Justin but the sound of him has faded. I think he may have left for work, but I know I did not hear his Jeep drive away. Still, there's not enough reverberation for him to be present. The empty absence of his void is tangible. I look for him with my ears until he becomes everything I hear in silence. He is not here but he is everywhere.

The bedroom door remains closed as I try to decide whether or not I can still move with everything inside of me broken. I decide I can't but I am full of piss without a catheter to drain me. I need to pee and as low as I am it would be lower still to lay in my own soil. I rise like a corpse from a grave, slowly, moving back towards life.

My dog bolts from the room just as soon as there is opportunity, but it takes a while before there is one. I can't get to the door fast enough, walking on crushed knees. Everything hurts. The pain has me buckling on bloody stubs, amputated of everything but nerve endings. I am nearly doubled over and falling down by the time I make it to the door which I hold onto like the last stand at the Alamo. I've been shot through the chest. There is a hole in the center where my heart used to be.

White knuckles grip the door frame. My face is flushed like I've been running from something mean, something that bites. Beads of sweat bubble up on my forehead before bursting like blisters that ooze instead of drip. I am a festering wound; open, bleeding, raw, a chunk of meat thrown in with sharks and then eaten alive. *I am not going to make it.*

The door falls open as if it were never latched as I step over the threshold of my room and into *his house*. Trespassing. *I don't belong here anymore.* The truth echoes back at me through my mouth until I am gagging again. Sick. I am going to be sick. I hold the vomit in my throat along with the breath I refuse to let go of. It's not long until I am choking on both, heaving forward.

I listen for my dog as I stand at the bottom of the stairs looking up. Lurking. I am a creature chained to shadows, burned by the light that creates them. I wait there then, in the dark below, with my ears turned and pointed. My dog is not there. Neither is he. The whole box is empty like the plane in the Langoliers. They've disappeared. Gone so suddenly it must be gruesome. *Where did my dog go? Why didn't I hear his jeep leave?*

I am afraid now in ways I haven't been before. *What if he is gone forever?* The question hangs there in the rafters above, a noose to strangle myself with. I know better than to stick my head through that twine, but I feel like I need to. *I need to find out what happened to Justin.* The urgency to know goads me until I forget all else, including my broken heart and mangled spirit. There is no pain when I step. No

25

agony. I am healed just as fast as I was injured. Panic has surely changed things.

I take the stairs two at a time and it is a healthy flight. If I am winded at the top I don't notice. All I can think about is Justin. *Where did he go? What do I have left of him?*

His watch is not waiting for me in a pile on the living room floor and neither are his metal fillings. *He didn't vanish like the passengers on the plane of the Langoliers.* A palpable relief sweeps through me, but it is temporary. The room is empty and normal with nothing out of the ordinary except my fear. The terror hangs on with talons.

The grim quiet is unsettling proof. Something is horribly wrong. I make my way to the front window and pull open the curtains. What I see next has me reeling. His jeep is still in the driveway. *He should be home.* I begin to tremble as I move through the remaining rooms of the first floor. Each one of them is empty and normal with nothing out of the ordinary except now my fear has mutated, a malignant cancer with cells growing uncontrollably. I am sure now that he didn't simply go to work. *I would have heard him leave.*

I press on to find him even though I am certain the discovery will be morbid. I check the bathroom. I check our bedroom. *It's his bedroom now.* I open the door to every closet. I look under every bed. There is nothing except the mute muzzle of the missing. I am alone when I shouldn't be.

The kitchen is the last room I check. It is there I spot him through the window in front of the sink. He is outside, sitting sideways on the picnic table that resides on the back deck, the same deck we torture our *other* dog with at night. *His dog---Elvis. The old dog that shits and pisses everywhere.* Both dogs are sitting with him, mine being a traitor. The sight of him is a shock I can't undo, but it is proof he is still living and not a science-fiction casualty.

Justin is not the victim of anything but bliss. He is looking down at his cell phone. It is lit up like his face which is beaming with delight, radiant with joy. His thumbs are moving rapidly, texting. *Who is he texting?* He takes a sip of his coffee. Laughing. He is drinking from a mug he brought me home as a souvenir this past summer. CALIFORNIA REDWOODS is stamped on the front of it--- An ironic insult to injury. He knew all too well how badly I had wanted to go with him on that trip. I had implored him to include me, telling him about a book my father had given me when I was a little girl, a book with pictures of trees so big you can drive your car through them, trees I have wanted to see for what seems to be my whole life. I had wept as I pleaded for him not to go without me. Then I sobbed as he drove away with his son. I went dry when he returned home with that cup. Any tears that might have fallen evaporated as I was incinerated by his callousness.

The iconic Sequoia 'Tunnel Tree' was toppled by a California storm a month after the vacation Justin would not allow me to enjoy with him and his son. I cried on that day. The day it was too late. The day I realized there would be no tomorrow. It didn't matter that there was still an entire forest to explore, other big trees. The 'Tunnel Tree' had weathered tempests for more than a hundred years but it fell soon after Justin brought that coffee cup home to me. I suppose I should have known I would be next.

I watch him from the window as I retreat back to the gloom of my room below the stairs. He is wearing a giddy grin which has not stopped the entire time he has been texting. *Who is he texting?* The questions nags but I know. *There is someone else.* He used to smile at me the same way, back when he was in love with me.

CHAPTER THREE: THE WRONG WAY TO EAT JESUS

Chapter Soundtrack: "Laughing With" by Regina Spektor

Lexi Kensington is having a dismal day. "I HATE YOU MOM." Her son is screaming at her from the back seat as she navigates traffic going seventy. She can see him through her rearview mirror. He is red like a baby hamster belly and just as ugly in the midst of his fit. They are late or at least it feels like they are. For her time holds the tension of a mouse trap. It is a vice that will break her back in half if she doesn't hustle, *so she hustles.* She is going as fast as she can, but it is not fast enough to escape the squalling tantrum of her only boy.

Maybe I should have had an abortion. She thinks to herself, feeling only mildly guilty because she *had been* considering it at the time it was an option. She found out she was pregnant with her first born nearly the same day she found out her husband was cheating on her with a nineteen-year-old bikini barista named Daisy May. *He likes to fuck me in the ass.* Daisy May did not care to keep things secret and she was sure Mrs. Kensington should know. *I will be sucking his cock tonight. What are you going to do about it?* She had broken the taunting news to Lexi via text message, complete with a photo of her husband's erect penis as further proof.

What a dick. Lexi did not know what she could do about her duplicitous husband and his vulgar mistress, but she was surprised to find she did not care. What she did care about was the baby now growing inside of her and the impossible choices she would soon need to make. *Should she keep it? Should she stay married?*

She had gone to church, a devout Catholic, to pray for God's guidance. She did not find him there. It was the first time in her life church felt like just another building, forsaken of any special power, a commercialized farce. She questioned her faith as she sat there on her desolate pew. She believed, sure enough, but did she believe in something that was never real. *Did he ever really love her?*

It was then she decided God and love must be the same thing- imagined to keep the living from becoming the dead. *Why would we continue on otherwise? What would be the point and with so much pain involved?* It took her some time to reason out the facts as they were, to let go of the good she believed she would always have. God had been a constant by her side, but now she admitted he was gone. The seat next to her was empty. It had always been empty.

Fifteen years later, her teenage son is a terrible toddler with too many hateful words in his vocabulary. "You are completely worthless. You do know that right?" Kyle Kensington has stopped screaming, but he hasn't stopped being mean to his mother. He kicks the back of her seat, hard, with the bottom of his heel. His shoe connects briefly with the small of her back, lurching her violently forward. The driver's seat shakes with turbulence. Lexi grimaces but does not react otherwise. She stares forward with a flat empty face, at the other cars in traffic---- the ones she's currently trying to avoid. *Maybe she should crash into one.*

"Hey stupid. Are you listening to me?" Kyle's first kick does not earn him any attention, so he kicks harder, raising his voice to yell at her again. "I *said...* I HATE YOU." This time his foot launches her into the steering wheel and she nearly does crash.

The car veers sharply and almost too fast for her to recover. Screeching tires and angry honking horns blare to scold her for being careless. She should have expected him to kick her a second time. She should have been paying attention. She should have been ready.

Lexi's head snaps around, a whip cracked. Ready arrives like a bullet to the face. She does not yell back at him. Her voice is eerily calm. "If you kick my seat one more time." She doesn't finish her sentence. She doesn't need to. Something about her tone paralyzes young Kyle Kensington. It's ominous and queerly mesmerizing. His eyes widen as if he is being choked. They bulge as his mouth falls open. Agape like a fish gasping on air. Out of place. Put in place. He knows he nearly caused an accident. He also knows his mother is more dangerous than any wreck. She is the worst crash he can get into. He yields, a yellow coward, with no green light for go.

Lexi arrives at the Tumwater Valley Country Club ten minutes shy of nine surrounded by a cloud of gravel and dirt. Her patriarchal prodigy is on time for his tennis lesson and she is ready for a drink, if only she could find a moment for herself, and it wasn't still so early in the morning. *She could have a mimosa. No one would judge her for that.* Her phone is buzzing on the dash of her Cadillac Escalade, ringing with another call she won't likely take. *How many calls has she missed?* She counts ten from the last hour, the last two being from her estranged husband. The current one being from me. She misses my call while she sits in a numb stupor considering whether or not she is *still able* to talk. Catatonic. She fears she's gone deaf, dumb, and stupid at the same time she embraces the possibility. *Maybe she should just shut herself off completely. Maybe she should just quit.*

My phone rings at nine o'clock even, ten minutes after my failed attempt to get through to Lexi. She's on the other end of the line, just barely. Her breathing is more audible than her voice, both are tepid. "You called me?" She asks like she can't be sure, even though she is.

"Yeah." I say, feeling equally put out, but also trying to hide it. "I was calling to see what you are up to this morning. Maybe we can get together? I have news."

"News?" Lexi's voice picks up, curious. "What *kind* of news?" She asks narrowly.

"Justin broke up with me yesterday. This time I know it's for good." I blurt out the truth as I know it, but Lexi refuses to believe.

"No way. He loves you Amber. He was probably just upset about something. I am sure you guys will get back together. You always do." Lexi is positive, always positive, even when the worst needs to be reckoned with.

 I don't bother trying to convince her further. I know she is wrong. There is no silver lining to the clouds above me, nothing pretty and hopeful to hang on to. The sky is dense with dreadful darkness. There ain't no sunshine. He's gone.

"I am heading to church if you want to meet me." Lexi offers as she speeds through a school zone. She's going forty-five in a twenty-five, oblivious to every potential hazard save one. She can't be late. Tardiness would be far worse than plowing over young children with her SUV. *She might actually enjoy running one down---* but she can't be late.

She mentions church. I balk. "*Church!?* I was thinking mimosas and bacon." I complain and suggest. There are a great many reasons I generally avoid church. The easiest being that I'm not good at it. I have a terrible time with ceremony. All ceremony. Weddings, Funerals, Graduations; all things formal. Reverent people freak me out. Groups of reverent people are simply unbearable.

Lexi swerves to avoid hitting a little black cat that darts in front of her, checking her mirrors to make sure it made it to safety. She sees no further sign of the cat, alive or dead, which spooks her. *Black cats are unlucky omens.* She thinks to herself before insisting church is necessary. "Trust me. I was just thinking about mimosas. I feel like I really need church today. You should come. It will do you some good Amber."

I want to tell her no, but I am compelled to agree with her. Church might do me some good under the circumstances, which are dire. I am desperate inside. The devil is winning, my soul nearly forfeit. "Sure," I hear myself tell her. "I'll meet you there."

Lexi is sitting in her SUV when I pull up next to her to park. She's on the phone. The expression on her face tells me she's having a conversation with someone she should have avoided. Her mouth is pinched, turned down at the corners in a disapproving frown. Both of her arms are flailing in short, exasperated bursts. She looks like a composer without composure, frantic to play a tune that's not off beat while missing every note. Whoever she is talking to has her undone. I can see she is on the receiving end of losing, locked in a battle of words that are cutting her down.

I don't wait for her to finish her conversation, nor do I allow it to continue as it is. I exit my vehicle to stand next to hers. She is so engrossed she doesn't notice me at first, but then I make myself impossible to miss. I stand at her window playing peek-a-boo with my tongue sticking out. I contort my face to make me look inbred and fugly, drooling. I bend my arms and scratch my pits. I jump around like a monkey wearing a little red suit, clanging on cymbals to start a happy dance parade. I try to cheer her because I can see cheering is what she needs.

Lexi doesn't give me the smile I am hoping for. Her face is blank as she holds one terse finger up at me to gesture. *Give me a minute.* I refuse though. I keep dancing, a clumsy comical spectacle, obscenely out of place amongst the reverential church goers who are passing by in the parking lot. Stoic solemn faces turn briefly to watch, as starkly pressed people invoke me to halt my absurd behavior with nervous, telling glances. *This is highly inappropriate. Highly inappropriate indeed.*

I realize I want to leave after I've just arrived. I don't belong with these congregating suits garbed in repulsive seriousness. This place makes me shiver, or maybe it's just the cold. All I know is my hackles are up like danger is coming. My instincts are telling me to escape while I still can. *I should have brought my rubber chicken.*

My fate is sealed by Lexi. She hangs up the phone as she floats down and out of her vehicle to join me for church. She is so light her feet seem to hover above the concrete, blithe like a fairy spinning in glitter. I am dazzled by her beauty and consumed by her pain. Both are equally glorious.

She is smiling with everything but her eyes as she acknowledges me with an apology. "I'm sorry to keep you waiting. That was Chad." She confirms my suspicion. She had been talking to her soon to be ex-husband, Chad the Cad.

 "He is refusing to pay his child support again. But enough about that. How are you holding up?" She dismisses her strife as if it's trivial compared to mine, reaching out to hug me. She smells like honeysuckle and lavender, fresh as the blossom of spring. She is meticulously manicured and pristinely put together despite her continuous maiming. I am a blithering mess by comparison, blatantly unraveling.

"I can't believe he broke up with me." My repugnant news echoes from the empty hollow of my chest; dull, flat, cracking.

Lexi offers a radiant refusal, taking my arm in hers. "I am not surprised at all. He breaks up with you all the time. Like I said before, you two will get back together. Watch." She assures me, an oracle of good fortune.

We enter the church as tiny aliens, abducted by the light. Myself squinting from the brilliant blinding brightness. Lexi's eyes are round and wide as she searches to see if he's returned. God is absent per usual, but the idea of him permeates. She remains hopeful as we make our way to find seats.

The room is nearly full, stuffed with people not quite so proper in that pause before church gets started. Humanity spills out of formality; a snotty faced toddler crawls on all fours on the seat next to his mother, a baby squalls without being quieted, an old man with a gnarly, withered, face snores like a Ford truck missing a muffler. As straight as they all are they can't avoid being bent.

"Are you going to take sacrament?" Lexi leans over to whisper right before the ceremony begins.

Her question is confusing like too many forks on the table at dinner. I chew on it without knowing how to swallow. *Should I take sacrament?* I don't rightly know the answer to her question and I'm afraid to ask. The whole deal makes me uneasy. "Are *you* going to take sacrament?" I ask, as I decide it's best to follow her lead.

She nods to confirm she will be partaking, dooming me to yet another uncomfortable undertaking.

I should have escaped while I had the chance. A tiny voice mocks as my heart begins to thud. I feels like I'm on a rollercoaster up on the highest vantage, looking down tracks so far under I can't see if a bottom exists. I know the coaster is about to plunge, that the fall is going to feel deadly. The tiny voice is now a screaming one, a pleading one. *Let me off. I don't want to be on this ride!*

Mass begins much like a parade, but without a happy dance included. People are blown out like candles being snuffed, hushed quiet by the glory of his Holiness entering the room. Puffs of white smoke swirl from a golden ball being swung from a pendulum as creamy white robes shuffle past pews of sheepy people. I am the black one in the group, bleatingly wrong, an outside intruder. I half expect the priest to call me out, but he passes by as if he has no reason to notice me. I inhale my relief, grateful to find I am breathing again, realizing I had been holding it. The room stands at attention, with worshiping soldiers ready with alms for all poor sinners. Every man, woman, and child now in full composure, regimented by ritual. Even the baby quits squawking, silenced dead like its mama done snapped its little neck. I scan for the infant across the room, relieved to see it alive and pink in the cradle of its mother's arms. It's a girl with round rosy cheeks and a round rosy mouth. She's pretty and still, a doll made out of porcelain. Her eyes stare forward, unblinking blue glass.

I am not exactly sure when I tune out, but I realize I am drifting before I go. *How much time do I have left?* My thoughts return to Justin as I grapple with the future. *What if he wants me out of his house in thirty days?* The question tightens around my throat, a vice made out of steel soldered to a ball and chain. It's heavy and thick, pulling me deep into a sea of doubt filled questions, all with answers I do not like. *I am going to be homeless.* I do not have enough money to move on from Justin. I *won't* have enough money. *There's not enough time.*

Lexi elbows me in the ribs to let me know it's time to pay up. An angelically carved altar boy is standing at the front of our row with a basket held out. There are folded green bills in the pile of collections, and I've got no more than lint in my pocket. I shrug at her unapologetically, thinking I should tackle the boy with the cash and take his money. Leave it to the church to ask for charity from those in need of charity. Lexi smiles at the kid as she contributes a crisp twenty, taking the basket to pass to me. I get rid of it like a hot potato burning hands, scowling foul.

The sermon drones on, a mundane and gentle hum. The father's voice is soothing, but uninspiring otherwise. I look to Lexi to see if there is any indication she might share my opinion. She does not return my glower. She is keen on the pomp and circumstance, ardently tuned in. The rest of the congregation is exactly the same, with one exception. The old man with the gnarly, withered face is back to sleep again. His snoring putters on in cadence with the droning preacher. His mouth is a black circle of open. His fleshy brown lips undulate with his escaping snuffle. He's louder than the service, but no one but me seems to notice. *It's weird that they don't notice.*

When you are strange, the world becomes an oddity--- A bizarre and freakish sideshow complete with crystal decanters of magical elixirs. *I wonder if they drug the holy water?* The people of church are morbidly mesmerized, entranced, and enthralled by a force I am not able to reckon with. I can't get on their wavelength, so I turn the channel in my head. My thoughts return to Justin and the life to come after, *what's next?*

I will need to find a place to live with a space large enough for an in-home photography studio. I do not have the funds to secure *both* an apartment *and* a commercial space for my business. I know I do not make near enough money to afford renting a house on my own. This means I will need to find a roommate. *A roommate that doesn't mind having a business in their home.* I have enough cash squirreled away to make the move in deposit, but I was saving the money for the new camera I need to keep my business running. My current camera is so old it's obsolete. The brand quit making it available for repurchase with so many new models following. I've been scrimping for close to a year to have enough to make my purchase, but I only have half of the six-thousand dollars I need. Now the money will be wasted on moving into a place I won't likely afford for long. The move is going to cost me my business. I will need to give it up to look for a job. *My business of thirteen years.*

I am years away in my mind when the room comes to life with movement. The disciples are rising in clustering groups, yielding in to form a line. Lexi is up with them. I startle to my feet to join, unsure as to what is happening. I shoot her a feeble questioning glance. I don't really want to know *what's next.* I am already horrified we are a part of it.

There are some who remain seated. I seek them out with jealous, forlorn eyes as I am pressed forward by the inertia of the biblical mob. *Why did they choose to stay seated? Should I have remained behind?* The line ekes onward, a conveyor belt of strait armed bodies and shuffling feet. I crane my head to find the front of it, so I can try to ascertain what the people are moving towards. The glimpse I catch is enough revelation. I pull back into formation. Communion has begun. *Why isn't everyone in line?*

The question nags like a torn piece of skin at the corner of a cuticle. I can't leave it alone, pulling at it until the flesh tears further and bleeds. *I should not be in this line. I have not earned the right.* I am struck intrinsically, with a knowing so profound it makes me dumb. It's as if God cut out my tongue so I would listen. *First you must confess.*

If I were to confess anything, it would be this---- I am a special kind of disaster. Botched debauchery. A complete and total asshole.

The ritual becomes clear as we make progress with the line. I no longer need to crane my head to see what is going on. A portly man opens his mouth to the priest, a wafer is placed on his tongue. He takes a drink from a chalice and then moves on. A woman with gangly arms and a long narrow face is next to receive, but she does not open her mouth the way the portly man did. She reaches out instead, taking the sacrament with her right hand, before bringing it to her mouth to eat. She also drinks from the chalice. The woman that follows her eats but refrains from drinking. *Why did she not drink the wine?* Lexi is up next and I am right behind her. She receives the Father's blessing with an open delicate mouth, sipping from the chalice the same way. Lexi Kensington is demurely graceful. She exudes sophisticated elegance. You can smell it on her, muddled with designer perfume.

I approach the Holy Father with all the finesse of a blind and drunken pick pocket. My turn comes before I've decided *how* I am going to receive my Jesus cracker. *Should*

I open my mouth? Should I take it from his hand? I stand before the priest, a stammering short circuit, completely unable to choose. *Get out of the line. I don't belong here.* The tiny voice is back--- too late. There is no grace to save me from the curse of being myself. I flit forward, erratically indecisive until the terrible end--- *and it is a most terrible end.*

The priest never has a chance to give me my blessing. I snatch it from his hands as if I am stealing back something stolen, palming the wafer instead of eating it. I decide I am going to chomp it down later, maybe even slowly. It's not often I have the opportunity to nibble on Jesus. I want to savor it, away from the mass of confusing corpus. I bumble past the chalice without taking a sip, nearly tripping on the robes of those offering, tangled by my own feet. *This was a terrible, terrible mistake.* My inner voice pesters. I push into Lexi as I try to get away, not looking back, urging the line to move. Something feels wrong in the worst kind of way. *I need to get out of here now.*

Escape does not come before the ridicule of a screeching nun. We are all caught in her horror, but I am trapped by it. "YOU! Stop where you are!" She cackles, a crow in black.

My back remains turned. I continue to push, but now the line isn't moving anymore. Everyone is stopped. Everyone is turned. *All of them are looking at me.* The entire congregation is gawping---- even the old man with the gnarly, withered face and the queerly quiet baby girl. Lexi is the worst of them. Her face is contorted into a mortified mask of condemnation. *What in the hell did you do?* I can see the question in her eyes, but I am just as confused as she is. It's abundantly clear I've caused a blunder. I am at a loss as to what it is.

"YOU MUST EAT IT NOW!" The nun hails on me hard, knocking me in the head with her demand as if she means to stone me to death if I won't listen, if I refuse.

I turn toward her, ready for combat, ready to run. "EAT IT!" The nun repeats herself. "You are holding the body of Christ in your hand. You need to EAT IT NOW!" She's irate, gesturing to the cracker I have clutched in my palm.

I consider throwing the offering back at her, but think better of it. I stand there instead, dense and doomed, weighing my options as if I still have choices. There is only one I can think of. *I need to eat my Jesus cracker. I need to eat it now.*

If you want to know how Jesus tastes I will tell you, he wasn't much for flavor. He dissolved in my mouth, mixing to spit, before I swallowed him down as a lesson learned. I was mistaken to think I could nibble on him slowly, later, away from prying eyes. The church needed proof I consumed him as they consumed me with damnation. Forever shamed through eternal life. Guilty of every sin. The wrong way to eat Jesus is to refrain from eating him at all.

> *"Truly, truly, I say to you, unless you eat the*
> *flesh of the Son of man and drink his blood,*

*you have no life in you; he who eats my flesh
and drinks my blood has eternal life, and I will
raise him up at the last day. For my flesh is
real food, and my blood is real drink. He who
eats my flesh and drinks my blood abides in
me, and I in him. As the living Father sent me,
and I live because of the Father, so he who
eats me will live because of me. This is the
bread which came down from heaven, not
such as the fathers ate and died; he who eats
this bread will live forever"* (John 6:53–58).

Lexi hugs me coolly as we part ways. The embrace is stiff, as if we are people made of wood knocking into each other. "I'll call you soon." She says before speeding off to meet her next obligation. I can tell her promise is a spoken pleasantry. She doesn't mean it. It will be more than a week before I hear from her again, and less than a month until we are no longer friends.

CHAPTER FOUR: WHAT'S THE DEAL WITH THE RUBBER CHICKEN?

Chapter Soundtrack: "Home" by Michael Buble

Driving away from church feels like moving towards heaven. I am glad to be free of the righteous conventionalism, and perversely amused by the scene I inadvertently caused. I hadn't intended to create a fiasco, but I should have known one would accompany me. There are great many reasons I generally avoid church. I am simply not meant for the institution. God has other plans for me. Plans that include a rubber chicken and everyone knows rubber chickens do not belong in church. It just wouldn't be proper.

Where do I belong? I drive without direction because I have no safe place to be. Justin will be home if I return to the house and I am not ready to face him. We haven't spoken since our break-up. I am afraid of what he will say, terrified he may want me to move out immediately. *I have nowhere to go.*

The truth is a taunting torment, but at least I am familiar with it. I've been homeless before and it was not the worst that's ever happened to me. The worst was losing everything AND my freedom. It was living life in a cage, a delinquent lower than the rights of man. It was not being clever enough to escape my circumstance. It was becoming a product of my environment, a cog in the system, a statistic of the losing kind.

I am not worried about being homeless as much as I am irked by the certainty---- after forty years of life I still have no place that is mine to belong to. I've got nothing to show after a lifetime of effort. *But.* I do have a rubber chicken and a rubber chicken is all I ever really needed.

I need to finish writing my book. The thought presses through the tangled mess of the others until nothing else seems important. The book has always been the answer, and yet after six years of writing I am still not close to finishing it. *And now I won't have time. I will be too busy trying to make ends meet.*

The clock on the dash reads two-thirty. The day is still pregnant with hours I will need to birth. I know I should be making the most of them, but the pain of the labor does not inspire me to push. I am too tired, drained listless by my broken heart. *My book is a stupid idea anyway. I am a fool. A crazy clown with a rubber chicken. Someone to laugh at, not with.*

My mind flips back and forth; positive to negative, negative to positive. It's true, my book is a stupid idea. It's also the best idea I've ever had and the key to solving my problems.

How to Make Ten Million Dollars with a Rubber Chicken.

Step One: The plan must be written down.

WRITE THE DAMN BOOK AMBER GARIBAY!

I know what I need to do in order to succeed, but I can't even make it past step one. Or so it seems in the moment. I let it be fleeting. Failure is not an option, but it could be my choice. In the end that's all that matters. I have a choice. I am not a victim. I am the result of my free-will. *What am I willing to do to make my dreams a reality?*

The answer is so agreeable I can't argue with it. I will write my book and the rest will be as it's meant to. My break-up with Justin was a devastating blow, to be sure, but it will only be the end of me if I let it. I cannot allow myself to wallow in self-pity like a pig stuck in the mud before slaughter. I have an example to set, a legacy to leave, a daughter to secure a future for.

She is on my mind as I pull into park near the piers of Percival Landing. I am eight blocks away from my decided destination, which is fine because I am content to walk. The day is mostly sunny with a chance of scattered showers, typical for Olympia, Washington in late spring. I am just lucky enough to have caught a dry spell, but not fortunate enough to have remembered my coat. The sun is shining, but there is no warmth from it. It looks like a cold copper penny hanging from a cloud; a small denomination nearly spent. The bulb dims further as I step out of my car, losing current as the wind syphons its energy to blow in surges of frigid gusts. I'm thrown back by the severity of the gale, then assaulted by spray from a passing car. The streets are still wet from a previous down pour and now so am I.

I want to go home.

I want to go home, but I no longer have a home to return to. I want to see my daughter, but now she will have no place to visit me. I'm in the midst of losing everything I need to be OK and I need to be.

I need to be OK. I need to be better than OK. I need to win.

I need to win so my daughter doesn't miss out on having a respectable mother, so she knows how to make a comeback if she ever finds herself losing at life, so she has a nest to return to if love ever abandons her. *I will never abandon her. I will be her rock. I will teach her how to build her own fortress, while I create miracles with my powerful mind.*

The life I imagine allows me to transcend the life I am living through, but I can't escape the reality in front of me, nor can I pretend everyone wins. My eyes are open to see the world as it is; I pass an ill-fated man who's made a bed on top of a mud puddle. He's tucked inside a sopping wet sleeping sack, curled in a fetal position on the concrete with his back to the wind. I wonder if he's warmer than the freezing I am, while wishing I hadn't chosen to walk to Batdorf & Bronson. The coffee shop is still some four blocks away, too far for me to make it without a coat. I'm in agony, chilled to brittle bones and clenched teeth. *I am going to die before I make it there. I'm going to freeze to death while waiting for the light to change.*

Death does not come as I expect it to, but I am tortured by the elements as punishment for my poor judgement. I had been stupid to think I could weather the weather. I hate being cold more than anything, and yet there is some small part of me that must have needed the pain. The deserving part. The part of me that knows I have it coming. *I am the product of my choices, not the casualty of circumstance.* I could have parked closer. I should have worn a coat.

Batdorf and Bronson is not a coffeehouse I typically frequent because of the parking. Capital Way is a busier street with only parallel options for those brave enough to try parking that way with so much traffic to navigate. *If there are even any spots available. It's rare to find one open.* I arrive to see I could have parked closer. There is a spot accessible directly in front of the business, if only I had been brave enough to try, instead of deciding beforehand that it would not be possible. *Why did I not choose to be brave?*

It's difficult for me to accept that I may have a pusillanimous character, but then my pattern of behavior lends proof. I've been avoiding parallel parking for as long as I've been driving because it's difficult and I am unwilling to practice until it becomes easy. I am afraid to try. The consequence being one that forces me to always take the long way around, costing me both time and comfort.

Arriving is a cherished comfort, and a relief gravely needed. I make it to the coffee shop in the nick of time, just short of perishing from the tempered torture of the icy wind. My hands are nearly useless as I fumble with the door before entering. I am unwilling to uncurl my frozen fingers from the knobby fists I've got them rolled into, so I bend and use my whole arm to loop through the door handle, pulling with my body while trying to gain leverage with my feet. The door budges just enough to allow me a hint of warmth, but my efforts are in vain. It's too heavy. I am helpless from the cold.

"Here, let me get that for you." His voice is a rich and inviting baritone, but I am startled by it none the less. I hadn't noticed his approach and he should have been impossible to miss. The man is tall and devilishly handsome, flawlessly tailored except for his roasted chestnut hair. It's tousled and casual, not quite messy, but far from deliberate styling. He's wearing a black double breasted pea coat and cashmere tartan scarf in shades of mossy greens. I am warmed by the sight of him, and then flushed scarlet by his long lazy smile and velvet eyes. It takes me a moment to realize he's holding the door open for me, that he's waiting on me to go in.

"So, what's the deal with the rubber chicken?" He asks, as we make our way into the enveloping warmth of the coffee shop. He motions towards my purse and the chicken poking out of it. The bird is bent in half, with two orange feet protruding and a beaky head stabbed out of the other side.

I smile coyly, spry with a secret best not revealed. "My rubber chicken is going to make me ten million dollars." I say, flirting shamelessly.

"Oh really?" He sounds surprised but looks interested. "How is that going to happen?" He asks in disbelief.

I laugh, taking my place in line to order drinks. "I am writing a book. You'll need to read it if you want to know how to make millions with a rubber chicken. There are certain steps that need to be followed." I make the proclamation as if the money is an assured and fool proof guarantee.

"What kind of steps?" He asks, wanting to know more than I am willing to elaborate.

"I bet you want to know all of my secrets." I tease him as we move up in line. "I already told you. You must read my book if you want those kinds of answers. I will share the first two steps with you though. If you want to make ten million dollars with a rubber chicken, you must first write down how you plan to do so. Then after that you must remember to carry your rubber chicken around with you. You won't make any money if you leave your rubber chicken at home." I share the first two steps with a stoic straight face.

He studies me as if he can't fully tell if I am being serious, before asking one last question. "When is your book coming out?"

"It will be here in time for Christmas." I set the deadline just as it's my turn to order coffee. "How to Make Ten Million Dollars with a Rubber Chicken. Look for it on Amazon." I say, before turning my attention to the barista.

I hope that I will see him again, but I never do.

CHAPTER FIVE: HE LOVES ME. HE LOVES ME NOT.

Chapter Soundtrack: "Grandpa" by The Judds

The book is not coming along the way I need it to and I am not making any new writing progress at the coffee shop. I can't concentrate with so much going on inside of me. *He never really loved me. Why is any of our story together worth mentioning?*

I am unable to come to terms with our ending. I had been so sure about Justin's feelings, sure of his love. Even now, after the betrayal of our break-up. I cannot believe he dumped me, and yet I had been expecting him to. Maybe I even encouraged it. I knew our time was temporary on the day he admitted he would never marry me. He let me know a few days before our third Christmas together, as I had made it clear, "The only thing I want for Christmas is an engagement ring."

He had responded by punching the wall and cursing my request. "I fucking hate Christmas."

I knew we were over then, but still, I prayed for a miracle. I prayed for love to win.

"This Christmas is going to suck isn't it?" Justin had worried as the holiday drew near. I remember feeling bad for him, but also the blame. I blamed him for ruining our happiness. If Christmas was spoiled, it would most certainly be *his* fault. Loving me should have been an easy gift, marriage a natural progression. I could see no good reason to deny me, and yet I knew he was going to.

"You are not being fair Amber. We have no business getting married. Our lives are going in two different directions. We want to live in very different worlds. I do not want to be married again. Knowing that does not change the fact that I love you." He had tried to make it up to me that Christmas morning, pulling me closer to explain. "I do love you Amber. I did not get you an engagement ring, but I did write you a letter." He pulled an envelope from our Christmas tree. The front of it had my name written in the middle of a great big red heart. The letter was typed out on a photo of our blended family; me and my daughter, him and his son, our two dogs, together for the holiday. He could not promise me forever, but he was able to paint me a picture of his love.

Amber,

I'm glad that we are together: you, myself, Sapphire, and Justice. Our "fake" family, but it is not fake. We're not that family that comes in the picture frame you buy. We are real and there is love.

Can't forget our dogs; Blondie and Elvis. I love that Blondie is the dog *version of you... calm and loving one minute and running around raging fire dragon like the next.*

Is this life so bad? I do not think so and it can only get better.

The Game of Thrones series official title is the song of fire and ice. Did you know that? I think you are the fire (Daenerys) and I am the ice (Jon Snow). Yin/Yang... balance...we are two sides of the same coin; opposites, yet parts of a whole.

I do not believe that the grass is greener on the other side and you are the only one I want. You do not need to worry about anybody else. You are not a placeholder. I am yours alone.

I love you. God bless you. God bless 'Merika' and Merry Christmas.

Your guy, Justin.

Four months later he was breaking up with me. He didn't mean what he had written. I *did* need to worry about other girls. *He found someone new, someone from Facebook.* I guess I was a placeholder after all.

I know Justin must still care about me on some level, but I also know his feelings for me will fade further as his new relationship unfolds. Whoever he is seeing is making him happy in ways I no longer can. I need to get my act together, and quickly. He may allow me to stay living at his house for a week or two, but he will want me to move out. I need a new place for both my home and my business. I also need to create an income I can rely on, as well as a budget so I know what I will need to earn in order to remain independent, in order to remain in business, in order to avoid needing a job, in order to avoid being *homeless*.

RENT: $1,900

UTILITIES: $700

GAS: $100

INSURANCE: $150

FOOD: $400

PHONE: $130

DEBT: $0

_____

TOTAL: $3,380

(Not factored in: Money for entertainment, Money for gifts, Money for vanity, Money for savings, Money for retirement, Money for investments, Money to run my business, Money to give to charity.)

The hurt I feel is consuming and dangerous. Maintaining the right mindset is crucial for success, but my thoughts are clouded with grief so thick all light is choked out. I am stuck in my dark despair, completely incapacitated by sorrow. I am not able to help myself and there is no one to rescue me. The truth of my predicament is quite severe. I am my only hope. I will rise or I will perish.

I think dying might be the easiest choice as I am devoured by the dour. Suicide becomes an option, though briefly. I flip it around in my head like a coin ready to be tossed as a gamble of fate; *heads I live, tails I die.* Except, I am not allowed to kill myself yet. I have work to do first, a ten-million-dollar plan to see to fruition. Death will come for me eventually anyway. I might as well see what I can do with the life I have left.

Gloom is what's left of the day. There is no trace of the sun or any breaks in the rain. I will be soaked if I attempt to venture back to my car, but I need to head home to face Justin. We need to talk about what's going to happen next, so I am able to plan accordingly. I am ready to move forward, or at least I think I am.

I change my mind soon after I am back out on the streets. *I can't do this.* It had been cold on my walk to the coffee shop, but now the rain has set in, now it's worse than unbearable. There is no way I will make it, and yet somehow, I do. I am drowned and drenched as I pass the homeless man still sleeping in his mud puddle. *How did he end up there? Why would he choose such a life for himself?*

I try to put myself in his shoes as I race by. I am frantic to return to the warmth of my car and refuge. There's solace in knowing I have those things waiting for me. This man has only a sack in a puddle of cold muddy water. I wonder if he's grateful. I wonder if he's grateful for the bed he's made himself. It could be worse. He could be laying there without any bed at all.

I am thankful to make it to my car, though you must know how much I loathe it. My car is not my favorite. My car is a ghetto hooptie ride. I feel like white trash every time I drive it. I am grateful the beast continues to run for me. It's a crap shoot every time I get behind the wheel. I never know when or where I am going to break down. She usually leaves me stranded in the middle of busy intersections, so traffic is obstructed, and I am forced to endure an onslaught of angry honking horns and near missed collisions as I am trapped in an unmoving vehicle with no one willing to stop to help. I hate my car and I am better for it. It reminds me to stay focused on my financial future.

The best (and redeeming) thing about my car is that it's already paid for. I do not have a car payment to make each month or any debt at all for that matter. Blessings, to be sure, but only temporary. I will need a new car and a new camera in the coming months. Both will require money I do not have, which means I will soon be broke and in debt. Unless I am willing to change.

Change is coming for me whether I like it or not. My life could easily spin out of control if I let it, but I won't allow my time left to be wasted that way. My plan will work as long as I don't give up on it. I may be low on resources, but I am already wealthy by what I know. I know how to make ten million dollars with a rubber chicken. Not many people can say that. In fact, I may be the only one who has.

Justin's Jeep is in the driveway. My stomach falls out of my throat when I see it. He's home and I am not ready. I am not ready to say good-bye to the man I love, but the beginning of the end has arrived. It will be best if I let him go cleanly and completely. There is no reason to love someone who does not love me in return. He broke up with me because he does not value the love, I have been sharing with him in our lives together. He does not value the treasure I am. He will be denied the wealth of my future. The loss will be his, not mine.

Except, the loss is mine and mine alone. Justin does not look up as I enter the house or give any indication that it matters to him that I've returned. He's on his phone, texting. I stand there in the entry, wanting him to notice me, but he does not, or at least that's how he makes it seem. He acts as if I am not there. It pains me to see him so happy in my absence, as I realize I won't be missed or pined for. He truly doesn't care. Our entire romance had been a farce, the fairytale of a fool. Years wasted. *How could I have been so stupid?*

"Can we talk?" I am the first to break the silence.

Justin does not look up from his phone, but he does acknowledge me by rolling his eyes. He's annoyed I am encroaching. "I guess." He answers begrudgingly. "What do we need to talk about?"

"How long do I have?" I ask him to give me a timeline, but he refuses.

"I don't know Amber." He is looking at me now. His eyes are cold stones.

I push to get some answers. "A week? A month? I need to know so I can make arrangements."

"I just told you, I don't know." His reply gives me nothing. "Maybe a few days. Maybe I will let you stay through the month. I haven't decided." He withdraws from the conversation after that, turning his attention back to his phone which is lit up with a new flurry of received text messages. He does not look up at me again. I am dismissed by lack of attention, abandoned to worry about questions with avoided answers. *Who is he texting? How long has he been seeing her?*

CHAPTER SIX: MY FACEBOOK STALKER STOLE MY BOYFRIEND

Chapter Soundtrack: "You Oughta Know." By Alanis Morrissette

Justin will insist he never cheated on me, but I can assure you he was never faithful. His first transgression occurred three years back, not long after I had fallen madly and mindlessly in love with him. We were a few months into our relationship.

"I think your man is seeing someone else." Lexi had called to break the news to me. "Have you been on Facebook?"

"Facebook?" I had asked, dumbfounded. I was on Facebook all the time, but I had missed the clues. My voice cracked as I tried to reply to a truth I was not expecting or ready to process. "Are you sure? Is she pretty?"

"You need to go look." Lexi had pressed. "But if it makes you feel better the answer is no. She is not pretty. She's old and haggard. Her neck looks like a turkey's nut sack. Her skin looks like worn leather and tobacco spit. Her forehead is huge. I mean bigger than Tyra's and we both know that Tyra Banks has a big forehead. I have no idea what Justin is thinking. She's got nothing on you."

"Really? Is she really ugly? How is that possible? Text me a picture of her." I couldn't believe what Lexi was telling me, yet she insisted.

"I will text you a picture of her, but you should just look her up on Facebook yourself. Go check out her profile and their comments on each other's pages. Justin is definitely cheating on you and if he's not he will be soon." Lexi continued to describe the woman she suspected Justin was seeing and the details of how I could find her, should I choose to look her up on social media. "Her name is Laurie and she lives in Longview. She's got little teeth that curve inward in the middle and big blue eyes that bug out of her head. Her hair is thinning and fried. It looks like she spent her life getting bad perms. She's not cute at all Amber. You are really going to laugh. I think she even has fake tits."

I didn't laugh when I saw the picture Lexi sent me by text message, though the woman was exactly as described. Lexi was right. She wasn't prettier than me, but it didn't matter. *Justin doesn't love me.* I was looking at her image, but all I could see was him.

It's funny how you can look at a person and fail to see them. When I looked at Justin I saw a man who loved me. Why did I see him that way? When it wasn't real? When it wasn't true? Or was it that I saw what I wanted to see? Maybe Justin never lied to me. Maybe he was faithful to the truth the entire time. His choices a reflection of his honesty.

Lexi had been right about Justin and Laurie. It was exactly as she suspected and worse. "Hi angel eyes. It's late. I am about to rack out, but I can't stop thinking about the last pic you sent me. I want to be inside of you…. Soon."

I found his emails to her later. After we broke up and got back together. Justin insists he never cheated on me because he broke up with me before he fucked her. He is wrong though. His infidelity had nothing to do with sex.

Justin did not really love me. I took him back because he wanted me to believe he did. He wrote me to explain:

> "Hey you. Well, one thing I can say about you is that you can always make me laugh. Every time I happen to see that key chain sitting on the table it brings a chuckle.
>
> One thing about each of us, I think it's easier to express certain things through writing. So I write.
>
> I get the feeling you don't want to talk about anything heavy, but some things need to be said. I didn't reach out to you for no reason.
>
> So why did I?
>
> I can tell you honestly, well, after things calmed down after our fight that I've thought about you often. And I've worried about you. Checking your blog

daily to see if there's anything new, because if there was something new it meant you were still around. When you stopped writing your blog I got worried. I reached out to your friend Lexi, trying to get information about you and how you were doing. At the time I thought it was just out of a genuine concern about your well-being and nothing else...but why should I care? If I dumped you like some trashy whore, why would I care? But I did care and I do. Was I worried about you because I feel responsible somehow for the spot you're in or because of guilt? People I've talked to have suggested that. That's something I've thought about a lot the last few days...if I care just because of guilt about hurting you or if there's something else too.

Arrgggg!!!

So. the person I've been seeing. She has really fallen for me hard, too hard and her feelings are pretty far ahead of mine. She is a really great person, good hearted and fun. She's also an Alpha female like someone else I know. Anyway, things have been going pretty good. She's in Longview so we have only seen each other I think five or six times. I do like her and we've been dating each other exclusively, but there's no commitment beyond that. Earlier in the week I told her about how I saw you on Friday and how I felt about that. She also thought I was just feeling guilty. I told her that yes, that's possible, but that it's also possible that there are still some feelings there. I told her that I couldn't move forward with her further, honestly, until I explored these feelings and tried to understand them and what they mean. She's giving me the time to do that and is trying to be patient.

You need to know that letting go of you was the hardest thing I've had to do, as far as relationship stuff. You think I just dumped you, but no, it was fucking hard. I kept wanting to go back to you and it was like weaning myself off of an addiction. I thought I had conquered it, but now not so sure.

I admit that I gave up on us too soon. When I was dating again after my wife and I split, I think I was just obsessed with finding someone who was exactly perfect. Problem is...no one is exactly perfect. I was too ready to stop things as soon as I found something I didn't like about a person. I've been thinking about you...your qualities and your imperfections...put them on a scale and it's no contest. You always say how awesome you are and it's true.

I feel bad about saying some of the things I said to you, like I couldn't see a future with us or I couldn't marry you. I shouldn't of pushed you away so many times. I had walls up and I never fully let them down with you. You never saw the best of me, fully committed and you deserved that.

We had our difficulties. There were things we needed to figure out with regard to how to deal with each other when we were upset about something and we never did figure them out.

You've mentioned family a few times lately. I know how much you want that family unit, You say that you think I want that too. Never really had that much that's true and that would be nice. Time is ticking by and it would suck to not experience that as others have. I had a waking dream a few days ago, a daydream I guess, but it wasn't forced. It just came to me. Anyway, it was a sunny day and you and I and Justice and Sapphire had hiked to the top of Mt. Ellinor, where Justice and I hiked last summer, and we're all smiling and happy. I took that as a prophecy or possible future that still could be.

But I'm lost right now and I'm trying to figure things out.

I'm sorry if all this has upset or confused you.

I'm rambling a lot. Sorry. Just a lot on my mind.

----Justin

I asked him later, while we are reconciling. "How did you meet her?"

"Facebook." His answer changed something inside of me. "She looked me up after reading one of your blogs. She follows you online."

"My Facebook Stalker Stole My Boyfriend." I laughed as I kissed his lips. "Now that is a great title for a chapter.

"She didn't steal me away from you." Justin tried to assure me, pulling me close. "I am here. I am yours."

Justin will insist he never cheated on me--- but he was never faithful. He says he was mine--- but he never was.

CHAPTER SEVEN: NEGATIVE NANCY CHOOSES HER FANCY

Chapter Soundtrack: "Fancy" by Reba McEntire

I am fat again. It's not as noticeable when I am wearing clothes that flatter my curves. When I get undressed it's a disaster. I've always had a large ass and small boobs. Now I have a huge ass, big floppy udders, belly rolls, and back handles. It's no wonder my boyfriend broke up with me. I understand love is supposed to be unconditional, but an erection is an entirely different animal. Erections require attraction.

How can a man stay in love with a woman he no longer wants to have sex with?

It's difficult to know what kind of man could be attracted to me in my current state. Maybe a man with a fetish for dimpled square bottoms or a man that enjoys soft squishy things.

To be fair, I am immensely hard on myself, but then that's just because I know what I am capable of. I would look and feel beautiful if I were taking care of myself, but I haven't been. I've been making the wrong choices. My weight is just one of many consequences. I am the product of my choices.

Why? Why did I allow myself to get this way when I knew what might happen? Why do I continue to sell myself short when I could be living my best life?

I need to change and this is not the first time I've come to this crossroad. I weighed just over two-hundred pounds six years ago, which may not sound like a lot to some people but to me it was devastating. I had become so fat I no longer recognized my own face when I looked in the mirror. It was a horror to see my reflection because I knew I had created the monster staring back at me. I had turned beauty into a beast.

Most of the people I know have a really hard time with the truth unless it's a pleasantry. They hate it when I am disparaging or downgrading.

I say, "I am fat."

They reply, "You are not fat! You are fluffy."

I lament, "Ugh. I can't stand the way I look!"

They reply, "You're beautiful!"

I say, "I want to kill myself."

They implore, "But you have so much to live for."

Society prefers me to keep negative things positive. I prefer to tell it like it is. When I say I am fat I do not mean it as a put down. I mean that according to science I am not maintaining a healthy weight. When I am fat it's because I am gorging on cancer causing junk food. I fall asleep with potato chip bags on my chest. I find melted chocolate in my bra. I drink wine like a wino. I drink rum like I am a pirate. Argh. When I am fat it's because I am living loose. Not all loose women are whores. Not all fat people mind being called fat.

When I mention I am not happy with the way I look, it doesn't mean I don't appreciate my natural beauty. When I am unhappy with my looks it's because I know I am not putting in the effort to maintain them. Gardens stay beautiful because someone cared to pick the weeds. I hate the way I look when I let myself go. I often deserve better than the love I give myself.

Suicide. Yet another truth people have a hard time understanding. For some people suicide *IS* an option. I happen to be one of those people. I will choose the way I live. I will choose the way I die. I am careful with my choices because the consequences will always be permanent. What's done will always be done.

Six years ago I began making plans to end my own life. I started making those plans at the very same time I decided I would make ten million dollars with a rubber chicken. *Why would someone with ten million dollars want to kill themselves?*

I refused to go on living if it meant I would need to continue living the life I was stuck in. *I would rather die.*

I would rather die than be fat, broke, and single. Except, I wasn't really stuck. I could change and if I couldn't, well, suicide was always an option.

It didn't take me long to lose the weight back then. I lost seventy pounds in six months by making small changes on an everyday basis. I kept an accountability journal so my choices were recorded and concrete. When I made the right choices my weight went down. When I fell back into old habits my weight jumped back up. It wasn't rocket surgery.

And now... I am fat again.

How stupid is that?

And now... I am single again.

Dumpy and Dumped.

And now... I am still broke.

Have I made any real progress in the last six years? Yes. I have not yet acquired the money I intend to make, but I have gained more wealth. My ten million dollar plan is not just about making money. It is about creating a life that allows me to flourish. Is money important? Absolutely. Money is a useful and necessary tool, but it's never going to make me happy. There are lots of unhappy rich people. I don't intend to be one of them.

Negativity shouldn't always be avoided. Sometimes it needs to be confronted and questioned. If you want to make ten million dollars with a rubber chicken, you need to be willing to face the truth of who you are. *Are you a wealthy person or are you a poor person? What makes it true? Are poor people negative people or positive people? What about wealthy people?*

I've heard people say money is not important. I won't disagree but I am imploring you to think about that statement. If money isn't important to you I suspect you won't have much of it in your lifetime. I can say this because I spent the first half of my life living by that philosophy. I believed love held the most value. *Money doesn't matter as long as we have each other.*

Do you want to know what's worse than suffering through a broken heart? It's losing the love of your life and everything you spent years working for--- all at the same time. That's exactly what happened to me six years ago, back when I was a ready to die fat chick.

First my husband of seventeen years told me he wanted a divorce and left me. Then I shut down my photography business, even though I needed the income, even though I was drowning in debt, even though I loved taking pictures. Soon after that I ran out of money and then out of food. I began selling off furniture so I could buy groceries for me and my daughter. Next, I sold our refrigerator because she needed a flute to participate in band at school. I didn't have the money to buy it for her and I refused to let her believe I simply could not afford it. The two of us lived as squatters in our own home through the foreclosure, despite daily threatening phone calls from the bank. "You have two more weeks Mrs. Garibay. We will send a sheriff to remove you after that."

I became a writer during that time of my life. I started writing this book you are now reading and a blog to build a following on social media. The very same blog that helped Whorie Laurie steal my boyfriend. I became a writer and lives were ruined (and saved) because of it.

FAT. I've been down this road before, but this time I can't quite get a handle on changing the behavior that created it. I make it to the gym a few times a week, but my body is still going in the wrong direction by appearance and size. Sure, fitness is helping me be healthier. The truth is still the truth. I am fat because of the food I cram in my mouth. Tonight I plan on bringing home Dirty Dave's pizza and I am not going to have one or two slices of the family-size Gay 90's Special. No. It's my all-time favorite pizza. I am going to eat half of the whole pie. Maybe more if I can fit it in. It's already been decided. I've been thinking about it all day.

I am thinking about the pizza I plan to eat as I try to get my jeans on over my bare behind. I do not wear underwear anymore. I stopped when size LARGE no longer fit me. I am unwilling to go buy supersized grannie panties. I am also unwilling to buy jeans in a bigger size. I already have five pairs and each one of them is the next size up. If I get new jeans, I will only grow larger.

I try to make the jeans work, even though I already know they are too small. I can get them buttoned and zipped, just barely, and only for a time. It's not long before the pressure of my bulging gut pops the button open and forces the zipper down. My muffin top cannot be contained so I abandon my jeans, choosing a pair of Loopy La La leggings instead.

The problem with leggings is they were never intended to be worn as pants. The material is see through thin, which means I need to find a shirt long and wide enough to cover the expanse of my ginormous behind. I try on several tops, but none of them work. Almost my entire wardrobe is now too small for me to wear. I bend over in front of the mirror to see if my ass crack is visible through my leggings. My rump looks like a lumpy bowl of porridge, and it's obvious I am not wearing any underwear. I can't leave my house looking this way. I will though. Nothing is going to stop me from getting my pizza. Dirty Dave's does not deliver. I will show up naked if I need to.

The disgust I feel as I scrutinize my appearance does not alter my course or change my plan for the day. I am not quite ready to change my eating habits, especially now that I have no one to look sexy for besides myself. My weight is fine for now, even though finding clothing is a problem.

It's true. Most of my problems are self-created. Admitting I am the problem is both empowering and debilitating. *Maybe I am just a loser?*

Aristotle wrote, "We are what we repeatedly do. Excellence, then, is not an act, but a habit."

If I am in the habit of repeatedly losing it's entirely possible--- I am a loser.

So, what now?

If I am a loser, I certainly do not intend to stay that way. I will remain in the race, working to best my own best, while striving to win. Or at least that's how I feel about life most of the time. Today I could give two shits. I don't care if I win or lose. The only thing I care about is pizza.

I find a Loopy La La dress in the dirty clothes. I smell it to see if it's salvageable even though I know I will wear it regardless. The garment doesn't reek, but it is soiled. The front of it is stained with food that somehow missed my mouth and there's a lot of it.

You look like a fucking slob Amber. Jesus. Pull yourself together. Is this really what you've become?

I chastise myself as I stare at my reflection in the mirror. I am a pretty woman, despite my attempts to ruin it. The outfit I've selected isn't paying me any favors, but I still manage to somehow pull it off, even with the globs of grease down the middle of my dress. I pull an infinity scarf from the top of my closet. It's too thick to wear in spring, but it will serve its purpose. I am able to hide the evidence. No one will be able to tell I am wearing dirty clothes.

I appear to be perfectly put together as I leave the house to go pick up my pizza. I know the truth though. I may have been able to clean up well enough to fool the fools, but there can be no fooling me. The person I am allowing is not the person I am meant to be. It's time to raise my standards before I succumb to passive mediocrity. Having a rubber chicken isn't enough to make it big. I will need to choose. I can live my life as a negative Nancy sob story or I can empower myself to enjoy something a little more fancy, a little more fun. A woman with a rubber chicken should always be fun. It's time for me to start living by my own philosophy. One choice at a time--- the battle will be won.

CHAPTER EIGHT: THE OTHER WOMAN CAN BE ANYONE BUT HER

Chapter Soundtrack: "Lies" by Marina and the Diamonds

A few days turns into a few weeks. Justin allows me to continue living with him. "Please promise me it's not Whorie Laurie." I ask him to give me a clue as to who he's been dating, but he remains tight lipped and secretive.

"If it's Whorie Laurie I will leave and you will never see me again." I warn him like my threat should sway him. I know better though. He doesn't really care if he sees me again.

"You promised. You promised it will never be her. You can't be in love with my Facebook stalker." I implore him to choose the way I want him to, but I know I am not a consideration. Justin does who and what Justin wants to do.

"It's been three years since Laurie and I had a thing Amber. What makes you think I would still be talking to her?" Justin implies that I am wrong, but I know better. I know he's stayed in contact with her. I don't have solid proof--- but I know.

"I mean it Justin. If you ever valued me at all you will pick another girl. I know you and I are over. I am cool with that. I know you are dating someone else. I am fine with that too. Whorie Laurie would be the ultimate betrayal. It can be anyone but her." I warn him again because I know. Whorie Laurie is back in the picture even if she is not the one Justin is fucking. I can feel it in my gut. She cannot be his friend or I will hate him. I do not want to hate him.

"It's not Laurie." Justin says before I am dismissed. "I will not tell you again."

I know the woman is not relative and unimportant, yet I obsess. I want to know. It doesn't really matter who Justin is dating. Justin is as irrelevant as the woman he is now banging, but I allow him to matter. I am holding on to him, hoping I am wrong, believing that he cares, and thinking we are still friends. I am holding on to a relationship that's not really there. Much like Whorie Laurie. She never let go. Nor have I. We at least have that in common.

"Are we friends?" I ask him because I do not know what we are. Now that we are broken up. Now that we are not a couple.

"Yes." He answers quietly. "We are friends."

"Will you be sad when I go? Will you miss me?" I ask, wanting him to give me some indication of what our relationship means to him, now that we have ended. Now that there is no longer any love between us.

"I will be happy you moved on. I want the best for you Amber. I truly do." He is kind, but I know better than to make it about me. He does not really care about what happens to me. He is concerned about being the better person. Justin Hayward wants to be a good guy. It's a great misfortune that he isn't. I want him to be a man he never was.

"He doesn't love you Amber. That does not mean he is a bad person." The voice inside my head is reasonable and fair.

The voice in my head can fuck off. Justin Hayward is a bad person and it has nothing to do with his lack of love for me. It has everything to do with his character.

I watch as he gathers his things. He's getting ready for work and I am ready for him to leave. It's dangerous when he's around. *Out of sight. Out of mind.* I am careful about how much I interact with him now. I do my best to make sure I am quiet. I try to be unassuming, to be small, but I am never small enough to be invisible. I am never small enough to be gone.

I need to be gone from this place that is no longer home. I need to get away from this man who does not love me.

Justin walks by in his underwear. He is not wearing a shirt. The shirt is in his hand because it's wrinkled. His shirts are always wrinkled in the morning. He never irons them, nor does he hang them while they are fresh. He leaves his laundry in piles. You never can tell the dirty from the clean.

He's headed downstairs to the dryer. It's a part of his morning routine. The shirt will go in the machine to fluff and he will come up to shower. It is the same every day.

Except now things are different. A few weeks ago I was flirting with him as he walked by. "Hey sexy. Do you need help taking off those underwear? I've got teeth." I had purred at him playfully.

He had laughed, and then winked. "Not today babe. I am running late."

He wasn't late, but he was predictable. Morning sex was never an option, and still I tried most mornings.

Today is not most mornings. Today I evert my eyes when I see him. Today I see his exposed flesh and there is no turn on. Today he is fucking someone else. I am sickened by the sight of him.

Who is she?

I wait until I hear the water running before I begin to snoop. I know better than to hack his laptop because I've done so before. He is will be expecting it, maybe even hoping for it. He will kick me out of his house if he finds me poking around in his business.

I can't help myself though.

I need to know.

Is he talking to Whorie Laurie again?

I check his bedroom for clues while he showers. The room is not anything like it used to be. When we were together I kept it clean and composed. When we were together our bedroom was stylish, with decorative pillows and bedding that matched. Now there is one raggedy brown blanket piled in the center of an empty mattress and one stained standard-size pillow without any case. When we were together the room smelled like fresh linen. Now it reeks of musk and dirty socks.

I hear him drop something in the shower, which is in the room directly next to the one I am trespassing in. I freeze, craning my head to listen. I can't get caught, but I am not ready to abandon my search. I hear nothing to indicate he is getting out so I continue. I tip toe to the trash.

I am not exactly sure why I think I will find the evidence I am looking for in the garbage beside his bed, but if I do it will be fitting. Whorie Laurie belongs in the trash. I search for her there, but all I find is torn up paper and chewed up wads of nicotine gum. Justin was able to kick his cigarette habit, but he never could rid himself of his addiction to the drug.

I rummage through his room like a tweaker searching for a crack rock, but I don't find any clues as to who the girl is. I even check his mattress for cum, but find nothing. There is nothing to indicate Whorie Laurie is still in the picture, but I know. She is around somewhere. I will find her.

Justin is predictable and so is his shower. It's strange to me. He is a man who frets about the state of our world and environmental fallout. He thinks there are too many people on the planet. People who squander and waste valuable life resources. Water for example. How long can a human live without water? A few days? Justin takes showers for hours, sometimes he sits in them when he can't sleep. He takes showers like life does not depend on the water he consumes while he berates other people for having too many children. Justin is a predictable hypocrite. I take advantage of it. His lengthy shower will allow me to find what I am looking for. I know the truth is hidden somewhere in his house.

His backpack.

I will find what I am looking for in his backpack.

My heart races as I unzip the outside pocket, but I discover nothing out of the ordinary. Two flash drives, some ChapStick, more Nicotine gum. I contemplate searching through the flash drives. There could be evidence on one of them, but now is not the time for that. Justin will soon be out of the shower and I will need to be back in hiding before he leaves the bathroom.

I open the main part of his pack. All is as expected. Work folders. The content of his backpack is benign. I was wrong. I find nothing about Whorie Laurie. Justin turns off the water. I am out of time to look. And then I see it underneath the folders.

A letter.

Two pages.

Hand-written.

Signed by Whorie Laurie.

CHAPTER NINE: YOU DON'T HAVE ENOUGH MONEY TO KILL YOURSELF

Chapter Soundtrack: "Jar of Hearts" by Christina Perri

A friend of mine told me once, "People who kill themselves are selfish cowards. Suicide is an unforgivable choice. If you ever kill yourself don't expect me at your funeral. I won't care enough about you to be there."

I remember thinking, "If you were there for me when I was alive maybe I wouldn't have killed myself. I died because I was alone."

Alone.

I am alone.

Whorie Laurie's hand-written letter is in my hand, but I haven't read it yet. I don't really care what she has to say. I am just glad I finally have the proof I was looking for. I am just glad my intuition was right. Whorie Laurie never went away. Justin has been lying to me for years. "It's been three years Amber. You are imagining things. Laurie and I have not been talking. She is not in my life. You are crazy." He said the blame was mine, that it was all in my head, but he was lying about that too.

It's hard to know if you are being lied to when you want the truth to be pleasant. People lie to hide unacceptable things.

Justin knows I will never forgive him for Laurie. He knows because we talked about it three years back. Back when he was begging me to give him another chance. Back when he was professing his love for me, while doing all he could to let me know she was a mistake.

"She means nothing to me Amber. You are the one I care about." He had spoken with such heart. I wanted him to be sincere.

"If you care about me and she really means nothing to you then don't talk to her again. Not ever. She is a home wrecking whore." I had been clear about my boundaries, just as I was concise as to the reason why. "She's a stalker. She reached out to you on the internet because she was reading about my life with you. Our happy life. You would have never even met if it wasn't for my writing, if it wasn't for my blog. She is the reason I almost gave up. She is the reason I almost didn't become a writer."

She is also the reason I almost took my own life.

Some people do not understand suicide. They can't comprehend what would make a person decide to give up. What could be so bad when even the worst is always temporary? All of us suffer, but most of us do not choose to die by our own hand.

Most of us.

Some of us don't make it.

47,713 Americans died by suicide in 2017. Suicide is the 10th leading cause of death in the United States. (Stats posted on the American Foundation for Suicide Prevention.)

I am writing this book for those who did not make it. Maybe my words will help the people they left behind. The ones that loved them. The people who are still looking for answers. The people who are trying to understand.

Why?

Why did you kill yourself?

There will never be an answer good enough. Suicide is not a mental illness. It's a choice. Some may argue it's a choice made under the duress of mental illness. I disagree. I was not crazy or sick the last time I thought about taking my own life. I was certain. I was certain I had lived through enough already. I was certain I was ready for peace. I was certain life would go on just fine without me. I was certain I would be better off dead.

Three years ago Justin broke up with me so he could start dating my Facebook stalker and now she is back again. This time is different though. I don't want to kill myself. I want to live to tell my story. I want to live so other people have hope. I want to live because I have hope.

"I don't want to die." I whisper those words to myself every day. "I love my life." I remind myself often and always out loud. It doesn't matter where I am or who is listening.

"You are always saying you love your life." A client of mine pointed out one day. "Do you really mean that or are you trying to convince yourself?" She had asked.

I really mean it.

I love my life.

I am also a person who contemplates suicide.

Whorie Laurie and Justin were together the last time I came close to taking my own life. He had broken up with me to start dating her.

"Do you really want to die Amber?" I asked myself the question as I stood there sobbing. I was in a grocery store. I intended to overdose on sleeping pills.

How many bottles do I need to buy? Two? Three? How many pills will I need to swallow to ensure I cannot be saved?

"Do you want to be saved?" The question was there soon after I answered the first one.

No. I do not want to die.

Yes. I want to be saved.

"You can live Amber. Please listen to me. You do not need to die. Please have faith. Don't do this. God will not give you more than you can handle. Do you believe in yourself? Do you believe your life has a purpose?" My mind begged me to find reason, but I had already decided. I was going to kill myself and nothing was going to stop me. Not even the people I love.

I called my family to say good-bye before driving to the grocery store. I called my brother first. "Fuck you!" He was pissed at me for quitting. "Go ahead and do it then. You dumb bitch. If that's what you want to do. You selfish cunt. Just do it. I am tired of your threats. Just fucking do it."

Tough love.

I hung up on him while he cursed his good-bye.

I called my daughter next.

"Hi baby." I whispered into the phone. "I just want you to know mommy loves you."

She was listening, but despondent, still angry at me for the divorce she blamed me for. It was my fault, always my fault. She said nothing, so I continued. "I am sorry I do not have a proper place for you to come visit me. I am sorry I let you down. I know you think I am a failure, that you are disappointed in me. I need you to know I tried. I really did try. I love you so much baby girl. I am sorry. I am so, so sorry."

I did not wait for her to answer. Click. The line went dead. I would soon be dead too.

Why?

What kind of mother would choose to abandon her own child? Sapphire was only ten years old, too young to be without a mother, but I was going to leave her that way. She would need to fend for herself in life. She would need to be strong.

"Strong like you Amber?" The voice inside my head taunted me as I tried to read pill bottles through swollen eyes. "What kind of example are you? You expect your daughter to have strength you can't find within yourself? Do you really believe she is going to be OK while her mom rots in the ground? You can't do this to her. You are going to ruin her life. Don't you understand that?"

I understood, but it didn't matter.

My time had come.

Today was the day I would die.

My phone rang. Divine intervention. It was my dad. My dad is never nice. His call would be the push I needed. His call would help me end my life.

"Hello?" My voice cracked. I could barely get a word out. My throat was strangled with grief. "What do you want?" The last part sounded like an accusation. I suppose that is what it was.

"I want to know you are OK." My dad's voice was gentle. It was not supposed to be gentle.

"I am fine dad. Everything is fine." I wasn't lying to him in that moment. My tears had stopped. I was at peace with my choice.

"Your brother called me." My dad said quietly.

"And?" I quipped.

"I want you to know I am sorry I failed you." My dad apologized. "I am sorry I can't help you." He blamed himself as he struggled to find the right words. Words that might save his only daughter. "I tried to be a good father to you. I tried to give you wisdom, and courage, and strength. I tried to warn you about life. To prepare you for the worst so you could face it."

"I know dad." My words were heavy, too heavy. I said nothing more. I did not have the strength to carry on a conversation.

We stayed on the phone together in silence after that. I knew he was still there. I could hear his breathing. He knew I was still there. He could hear the sound of pill bottles as I pulled them from the shelf.

"I don't know how many pills I need to take." I said finally. My voice was flat and empty, hard, like an open hand slap to the face.

"You better make sure you take enough if that is what you are going to do." My dad gave me his best advice. "I wish you wouldn't though."

"Fuck." I replied, exasperated. "I can't believe they charge so much for sleeping pills. You wouldn't believe it dad. They want nearly ten dollars a bottle."

"I can believe it." My dad remained steady and surprisingly warm. "It's greed Amber. What the fuck do you expect? That's big pharma for you."

"I only have enough money for two bottles." I said, in disbelief. I had a twenty dollar bill with me. I no longer owned any credit cards. "Is there sales tax? I don't think I have enough for two bottles if there is sales tax."

"Yes, there is sales tax." My dad informed me. "And I would buy three bottles if I were you. I don't know if two bottles will be enough. You don't want to half ass it and wind up a brain dead vegetable." He warned me to be wary of a botched suicide attempt. He did not try to talk me out of my choice. If I wanted to die he was there to support me.

"You have got to be fucking kidding me." I said, laughing my loathing. "I can't even afford to kill myself. How pathetic is that! God dammit dad. I am a fucking loser."

"Yeah you are." My dad agreed with me. "Is that really how you want to go out? You want to die a broke loser?"

"No, fuck that." I said, putting the bottles back on the shelf. "This is not how I will end. I am better than that."

"Then act like it Amber. Pull your head out of your ass. Quit behaving like a spoiled rotten child. I raised you better than that." My dad was still kind in his honesty. "You are not entitled to anything. Remember that. You will have what you earn."

My dad stayed with me as I walked out of that grocery store without the poison I intended to buy. It was the last time I ever came close to killing myself and it will remain that way. When I die it will not be by suicide. I value my life too much to squander it and besides, I am going to make ten million dollars with a rubber chicken. Living large is rich revenge.

Three years ago Justin broke up with me so he could start dating my Facebook stalker and now she is back again. This time is different though. I don't want to kill myself. I want to live to tell my story. I want to live so other people have hope. I want to live because I have hope.

But still.

I wonder...

Who is Justin seeing?

Is the mystery woman Whorie Laurie?

It is time for me to read her letter and then after that I will go. I will not be home when Justin returns. He will never see me again. He will return to an empty house and Whorie Laurie's letter. He will have what he has earned.

"Dear Justin,

My heart was racing when I read your last email. First let me say I am so sorry about the "unauthorized mail" I sent to your work. I hope this letter does not get you into any trouble with your employer. I was terrified to reply to your email because I was afraid Amber might intercept it. It seemed safer to write you back long-hand and mail my reply to you. I knew I couldn't mail it to your house so I sent it to your work instead. When I called to get the address, I asked the very nice man on the phone how to direct it to you and when I said Justin Hayward he responded pleasantly, "Oh Justin!" And I told him exactly what I was mailing and he didn't tell me I couldn't do it. So I just assumed that meant it was fine. Again, my apologies if it caused any problems at your job. I am glad you reached out to me. And yes, I know Amber has had an unhealthy fixation on me. I have never held her feelings of hate and animosity towards me, against her. Instead, I've always chosen to try to put myself in her shoes and

*understand why she might feel the way
she does. You are right, I never did
anything wrong and I think she does
know that despite the fact that she
likes to tell everybody that I sent you
naked pictures of myself after we broke
up and that I kept pursuing you. I think
had she never read any of our emails or
communications or been privy via you
any of our history then I don't think it
would've been as bad as it is. When you
can actually read two people's
connection or chemistry or whatever
you want to call what we had, then
that makes it way more real don't you
think? I could only imagine how I would
feel having read all that or knew all
that. That was her choice to invade
your privacy so that's a consequence of
her choice, but I can still empathize
with how that had to sting. I am
definitely not the only person you have
been interested in since knowing her
but perhaps the only one where things
went to such a certain level quickly.
How are things going with Jenny?
That's the name of the girl you are
seeing now? Right? I can understand*

you saying you aren't in a rush to make anything serious. But how could you with Amber still living in your house? Anyway, I wanted to write you back and to let you know I am glad we are talking again. I sent you a friend request on Facebook. I noticed you and Amber are not friends online anymore. I figured it would be safe enough to connect with you that way. I've missed you Wally J. Let me know if things do not work out with Jenny. I would love to see you again.

All my love,

Laurie

Jenny.

Justin loves Jenny.

I know Jenny. She's one of Justin's Facebook friends. They went to high school together. I commented about her back when we were still a couple. "I think your friend Jenny has a crush on you. She is always the first to like and love your Facebook posts."

Justin had laughed, making light of my prediction. "She is just a friend Amber. There is nothing more between us."

"There is nothing more between us." I repeat his words as I get in my car to leave. I do not look back. There is nothing left to see.

CHAPTER TEN: THE DEMISE OF LEXI KENSINGTON

Chapter Soundtrack: "Concrete Angel" by Martina McBride

Justin Hayward is a man with secrets. Justin Hayward is a man with shame. It's a shame I won't warn Jenny. She might want to know her life is at risk, but I won't warn her. No. It's none of my business.

I do not bother packing before I leave. There is no point in trying to take anything with me when I have no place to go.

My choice to leave is not a smart one. I know this, but my pride insists. Whorie Laurie is a deal breaker. She is back and I am gone. Justin will never see me again.

I do not take my belongings, but I do take the time to remove the parts of me that make his house look like a home. I start in the bathroom. I pull down the curtains I hung to hide the drywall. His house was a place of half-assed improvement attempts before I moved in to decorate. I want to leave it the way I found it--- in shambles. I want him to come home to an empty box without any love inside.

I loved him.

I loved him despite his secrets.

I loved him despite his shame.

It is a shame Jenny doesn't know who he really is.

It is a shame no one does.

I drive without direction. *What are my options? How much money do I have?* Five hundred dollars cash. I have enough money to stay in a hotel for a few days and then what? It would be smarter to hold onto my money, sleep in my car. I can't afford a roof over my head and now I have no place to run my photography business. Leaving Justin's house was a costly choice. I didn't just leave my home. I lost my place to run a studio. I sacrificed my business for pride and principle. To prove a point. *He's going to miss me when I am gone. I'm going places.*

I know I am going to make it. I know I will succeed. I will make ten million dollars with a rubber chicken, but right now my resources are limited. Right now I need the help of good friends. Lexi Kensington is as good as they come. She's been my best friend for some time, though it seems like she is still avoiding me. I don't think she's forgiven me for church, which is odd as church is supposed to be forgiving.

Maybe it's not me though. Maybe Lexi's been busy with her own shit. I remind myself the world does not revolve around me, while knowing the universe is open to my great big plan. I just need to stay the course, but it's hard to stay on a path no one else sees. *"Go get a job Amber. You need cash flow, not a rubber chicken fairy tale."*

I may need to get a job now that I no longer have a place to run my business. I may even want to get a job after I finish writing this book.

After.

This book is the beginning of everything. This book is the blueprint that will change my whole life. This book is money I will make.

If.

If it is written.

I need to write the book.

But.

How do I write about Lexi Kensington without betraying her? How do I write about Lexi Kensington without ruining our friendship?

And.

What about Justin and his secrets? Do I have the right to let his skeletons out of the closet? What if he kills himself? What if he kills me?

People have died for less. This story will have real life consequences, even if it is fiction. Is it fiction though? I didn't intend it to be until it needed to be.

I don't know how to write about Lexi without losing her forever. It matters to me. She matters to me. I don't want to lose her as a friend, but that's exactly what's going to happen when this book drops. She will hate me for the rest of her bitter filled life. She may even hate me more than anyone, but it will never come close to how much she hates herself.

Lexi Kensington despises the person she's allowed herself to become. She hates that she is hateful. She hates that she is vindictive. She hates that she is shallow. She hates that she is mean. She hates to feed the hate inside of her, but it's insatiable. Her hate is a beast of consumption. It takes all she has, until there is nothing left but more to hate.

I love Lexi. She can't see herself through the hate, but I do. She's a flower being strangled by weeds. She's a flower with thorns shaped like monster fangs. She's the devil wearing Prada with a Gucci straight jacket. Lexi is the wrong that happens with big money. She's a high-society bitch. She's a social back stabber. All of her evils are necessities. She uses them to accessorize her hate.

Lexi Kensington is my very best friend, but that does not mean she really cares about me. She can't care for me. Her hate won't allow it. She is my friend because of what she gets from me. She is my friend because of my light. She is my friend so the darkness doesn't take over. Sometimes I think it might.

I try to call her to let her know I am coming over, but she doesn't answer. She hasn't answered any of my calls lately, which is weird because we used to talk several times a day.

Maybe she's mad at me?

I have a terrible habit of making myself the reason for all problems. I assume Lexi has been absent because of something I said or did, inadvertently. I can't think of any good reason though. If I did something wrong I am not yet aware of it. As far as I know we are still solid friends.

It's difficult to adjust my mindset, to find security in what I know to be true of the past. Lexi and I have a sorted history, but I assume the best as pull into her driveway. I have faith in our friendship and the love we have for each other. I've always been there for her and she's always been there for me. I call her an angel on earth because that's the kind of person she is. Lexi will do anything for the people she loves. I am people she loves. I trust in that.

Her house is one of upper-middle class grandeur. A new build in the best school district. Pricey. It reminds me of the house I lost in my divorce, minus the character and charm--- but then I am partial to my old house. It was the house of my dreams, while hers looks like it was built by Stepfords. Her house is submissively pleasing. It conforms to community code, which is perversion perfect. Nothing stands out in her neighborhood. All of the lawns are greener than the grass on the other side of the fence. Every home is immaculate. Every property pristine. Lexi's house is beautiful because it fits the picture perfect image. Her house is a Tiffany blue box without real people inside. Real people do not belong in her lifestyle.

Where do I belong?

I am an outsider as I climb the steps of prosperity. I am as small as a shrunken Alice as I raise my hand to knock on a door built too large. The door is taller than any human could be and impenetrably dense. Red knuckles with no sound. Any knocking I do is in vain. The inside doesn't really want to let the outside in, the door is proof of that.

I press the doorbell instead, which booms like a choir of grandiose church bells.

And then, I wait.

I wait to see if my friend will arrive to welcome me.

The door remains closed. Lexi does not come.

Maybe she doesn't know I am out here?

My finger hovers over the doorbell. I could easily press it again, supposing she hadn't heard it the first time. I know better though. Her doorbell is pervasive. There is no way she could have missed it.

No one will miss you when you are gone Amber. Go away.

Doubt and fear turn to dread as I realize I have been abandoned by my closest friend, and while I am already wounded. I have other friends I can turn to, but I won't. I can't let people see how badly I am losing because I know that is all they will remember. My circumstance will ruin any value I hope to have in the future. It will become the way I am identified.

Kindness shouldn't be a charitable action, but that is how it feels as the front door swings open and Lexi steps over the threshold. The goodness she offers is gloating, dutiful, and chaste. Charity because it's the right thing to do, not the want thing to do. She preferred to keep the door closed, but God insisted she let me in.

"Oh my goodness. I've been meaning to call you!" Lexi says. Her smile is warm and inviting. She hugs me. The embrace is stiff, as if we are people made of wood knocking into each other. "Come in. Come in." She says as she ushers me inside.

Inside is not the way I remember it. It's been awhile since I have been to Lexi's house. She's been busy. Busy removing Chad's decorating.

"Come see the bathroom." Lexi gushes past any awkwardness, taking my arm in hers. "You have an eye for these things. I want to know what you think."

The room is scarlet red and royal blue. Vivid. Wild. Flowery. It is happy like Crayola crayons orgasming new shades of color. Chad would hate it, but then Chad does not approve of anything Lexi does. "Wow." I say, smiling at my friend. "It's spectacular."

Lexi looks both relieved and hopeful. "Really? Do you really think so? You don't think it's too much?" She asks as if my approval might change something.

"I love it." My answer is honest, but I would have lied if I had needed to. "The wallpaper you chose is absolutely perfect. It's vibrant and beautiful, much like your soul."

"I was worried it might be too busy for such a small space." Lexi admits, wringing her hands together. "Chad would have never let me do something this crazy."

"Has he seen it yet?" I ask.

"Yes, a couple of days back. He came by to pick up Kyle for his weekend. Walked through the front door and the first thing out of his mouth was 'Jesus Christ Lexi. The house looks like shit'----and that was before he saw the bathroom." Lexi says, biting her lip as she continues to flit nervously. "He says the bathroom looks like it belongs in a whorehouse. That it looks gaudy and cheap. Then he told me it is exactly the kind of thing he imagined I would pick. He said it's ugly, just like me."

"I agree with him about one thing." I say, reaching out to grab Lexi's hand. "The wallpaper is the perfect choice. It is very much you. It's surprising and bold. It's sophisticated and complex. It's radiant. It's beautiful."

"I've missed you." Lexi takes my hand in hers, while pulling me in for a hug. We bump into each other like awkward teenagers trying to dance for the first time. "I do love you. I hope you know that. I am sorry I've been ignoring your phone calls. I just have so much going on. I couldn't deal with one more thing."

I cringe to hear my friend describe our conversations as "one more thing to deal with, but at the same time I understand. Lexi's stress makes my stress seem trivial. She's in the middle of a divorce. Her business is nearly bankrupt, her son treats her like a plantation slave, and the last I knew she suspected her boyfriend of cheating.

"How are things?" I ask, studying her face. She is still wearing the smile she greeted me with, but the cracks by her furrowed brow are telling. She's been crying under her mask. Her grin is muddy. Her eyes filled with pain.

"I can't even talk about it." Lexi manages to say before the tears break through. "It's too much."

She holds a hand up, as if she's bracing herself. She turns her face to heaven, blinking back the proof of her bleeding spirit, willing herself not to cry.

But then she does.

Lexi Kensington cries and cries.

I watch her weep, without taking action. I listen to her strangled sobs the way a priest does at confessional. We are both absolved by his mercy. Her tears are the gift of release. I watch her cry and I think about the rain washing things clean. There's a storm raging inside of my cherished friend. It sets her on fire till she's roasting in hell from the inside out. Until the rain comes. Until she cries and cries.

"I am sorry." She says finally. "Can I offer you something to drink? Are you hungry?" Lexi moves past herself to refocus on me.

I allow her the distraction. "Yes. I would love something to drink." I say, following her into the kitchen.

Brazilian cherry cabinets and slate colored granite have been replaced. Lexi's kitchen looks nothing like Chad's. The countertops are a dazzling white stone with delicate black marbling. She chose clear glass tile for the backsplash. I am not sure how I feel about the tile, but I am memorized by the pallet. The space she created is stunning and fresh, while Chad's style is classic conservative. His is expected, while hers is innovative.

"You are coming alive." I speak to the room as if it's an extension of Lexi.

"Do you like it?" Lexi asks. "What do you think of the tile?" She knows her choice may not be well-received. She knows because Chad did not like it.

"I wasn't sure how I felt about the tile at first, but that's just because it's unusual. It's iridescent. It almost seems to change color depending on the way the light hits it. The room is gorgeous Lexi. You have a gift for design." I reply. The compliments come easy. I am impressed.

"Wine or coffee?" Lexi offers from the vantage of her open fridge. She pulls trays of pre-cut vegetables as she nods toward the pantry. "I've got lots of healthy food, but help yourself to some snacks."

I take her up on her offer to indulge. Lexi's pantry just happens to be one of my favorite places on earth. She keeps it stocked with every goody you can imagine. There are cookies and cakes, chips and crackers, nuts and candies, doughnuts and butter rolls. I count six boxes of sugar cereal, three of which just happen to be my childhood favorites. Cookie Crisp, Lucky Charms, and Coco Pebbles. Lexi's pantry is fat girl paradise, and I am a chubby chaser.

"Wine." I say, as I grab a bag of Cheetos from the shelf. "Do you have a Cab?" I ask, because if she doesn't my choice will change.

"Yes. I have six bottles of Cab." Lexi replies, gesturing to her wine rack. "Feel free to pick your favorite but leave the bottle on the end. That's our anniversary wine. I plan to drink it on the day our divorce is final."

"How is that going?" I hesitate to broach the subject so soon after she's gained composure, but I suspect the majority of her tears were not for her estranged husband.

"He is refusing to pay his child support and he's claiming his business is not making any money. You know, typical divorce stuff. Kyle's tuition is due at St. Mikes, but Chad refuses to pay it. He told me to put our son in public school. Can you believe that? He actually thinks I would allow something so absurd. Kensington's do not go to public school. Everyone knows that." Lexi says her name like it's a noteworthy brand. "I expect him to continue to maintain the lifestyle our child is accustomed to."

I wonder about Lexi's pampered entitlement as I pour myself a glass of her wine. She talks as if she earned the money Chad is keeping from her and I suppose she has, by penance. Her husband's money was a choke collar around her neck during her marriage. He kept his bitch in agreeable submission by allowing her every tangible luxury. She was the best money could buy, but she was bought so he treated her that way. He paid for the privilege of hurting her and then he made an art out of it.

"What about James?" I ask about her boyfriend, hoping for better news.

"I got him fired from his job." Lexi admits. She reveals the news with a smug smirk. I can tell she does not feel bad about it.

"What!?" I ask, flabbergasted. "Wasn't that the job you helped him study for? It took him a year to land that job. Why would you take it from him?"

"Me?" Lexi retorts. "He did it to himself. He should have known better than to mail panties to female co-workers. I called every girl on his work roster before I called his boss. I got him fired, but he created the reason for it to happen."

"How many girls did he mail panties to?" I ask, both in amusement and intrigue. "And did you find proof that he is cheating on you?"

"Six girls." Lexi is forthright. "But no cheating. It's the strangest thing. He gets off on buying women pretty panties. It's disgusting."

"Did you break up with him then?" I ask, perplexed by the absurdity of it all. "I know he loves you Lexi and if he isn't actually cheating..."

Lexi cuts me off. "You think his behavior is OK? Really Amber? I went through his phone. He's been messaging other girls. He still has his dating apps active. And you don't think that's cheating?" Lexi yells at me.

I am the eye in her storm. I remain calm. "I didn't say it is OK. I simply stated what I know to be true. James loves you. I wish you two would stop playing games with each other and embrace what you have. I am clueless as to how to deal with his panty fetish, and I don't know anything about the other girls he's talking to."

"You are right. You don't know shit." Lexi continues to berate me for my assertion about James. "You think that's love? You really are twisted. He doesn't love me. He loves the things I buy him. He loves the roof over his head."

"Is he still living with you then?" I ask. "Why are you helping him if he is just using you?"

"I've been making him sleep outside in his car." Lexi says. "I let him come in to shower and make himself food." She speaks of him flippantly, like he's a tool and not the man she loves. "And besides, I need his help at the restaurant.

118

Two of my employees quit last week. He's been working their shifts while I interview possible new hires.

Lexi owns a popular restaurant franchise and once upon a time James was her full-time employee. That was before they fell in love in the walk-in cooler. Their working relationship could not survive the emasculation, nor could their romantic one. Lexi treats the help like minions. James was no exception, though he was her favorite lowly servant. He quit working for her to retain and regain some semblance of masculinity, while she continued to bust his balls daily regardless of employment status.

James is ten years younger than Lexi and not nearly half as smart. I am being generous by implying he is intelligent. He is more brawn than brain. He is exactly what a cougar trinket should be. He's fast, fit, and fuckable. A sexual workhorse. Lexi is in love with his dick, but hopelessly bored by his mind, and perpetually irritated by his boyish incapability. James is a bumbling mess of failure on nearly every front, but Lexi refuses to let him go. "So, you finally broke up with him?" I ask, broaching the subject once again, despite the possibility of more of her raging retribution.

Lexi rolls her eyes and sighs. "No, I did not break up with him. I love him Amber." She says the last part like it's hopeless. "How are things with you and Justin? Did you get back together yet?"

I scoff, burying my nose in my wine glass. I do not sip. I guzzle. "We are never getting back together. It's over. I told you that at church." I reiterate what I've already told her. "He has a new girlfriend already."

"What!?" Lexi is shocked by the news. "No way! I don't believe it. Aren't you still living with him?" She asks.

I polish off the rest of my wine in one gulp, pouring more as I reply. "I moved out today, well mostly. All of my stuff is still at his place. He doesn't know I am gone yet. I left after I found the letter."

"What letter?" Lexi asks, raising an eyebrow. She follows my lead with the wine, gulping the last of hers down, pouring more.

"Whorie Laurie is back. She mailed a hand-written letter to his work." I say.

"No fucking way. They got back together? She mailed a letter to his work! That is so bizarre. Doesn't he realize she's a whack job?" Lexi exclaims. "I can't believe it."

I nod, holding my glass out to her to clank. "Cheers to new beginnings." I say.

She extends the toast. "Cheers to not so happy endings. At least you are not trapped anymore. Do you think he's been seeing Laurie this whole time?"

I shake my head, "No, Laurie is not the girl he is dating now. She mailed him a letter, but they are not messing around as far as I can tell. He's dating Jenny."

"Jenny? From Facebook?" Lexi's mouth falls open in shock. "You told me you suspected something was going on between them, but I honestly thought you were just being paranoid because of your history with Laurie. What in the hell? He insisted they were just friends."

"They are friends." I agree with her. "Friends with benefits."

"What are you going to do? Where are you going to go? What about your studio? Oh Amber, I am so sorry. I didn't realize it was so bad. I should have been there for you. I should have answered my phone." Lexi laments as she settles up with the truth of my predicament.

I pull the cash from my pocket and lay it on the counter. "I was hoping you could help. I know your finances have been stretched thin because of your divorce. I can give you $500 if you will let me stay here for a month. I need a stable place to crash while I look for a new place. Truth be told, I left without a plan. I do not have anywhere I can go."

Lexi pulls her glass back, along with her kindness. She shakes her head. "I am sorry. I can't help you. I hope you understand, but I have a family to protect. If I take your money you will be legally considered a tenant. I won't be able to ask you to leave. I can't put myself in the position."

"You have a family to protect?" The question falls out of my mouth as a numb mumble. "You can't put yourself in that position?"

Lexi takes a sip of her wine. Her pinky finger extended. "I know this is awkward, but I need to do what's best for my family right now."

I stand, pushing my wine glass away. I take my money back as I stare down her demon. "You were my family before today." I say. "And you will be my family after because that is how I love my friends. I love them like they are family. I hope life never humbles you the way it has me. I hope you never find yourself in the position I am in now. I hope you never need to ask for help, but if you do, I want you to know my door will always be open. When you fail at life, and you will fail, I want you to know I will be there for you, even though you were not there for me. My door will always be open. You can count on that."

"You think I am going to fail?" Lexi seethes, as the storm rages on. "There is only one failure I see and it's not me. I have a beautiful home, and a business. I am a success. I am not the one with no place to go, you are Amber. You are the failure." She cuts at me before lunging in for one last jab. "Your door will always be open? That's laughable. You don't even have a house. How could you possibly have a door?"

"You are a terrible human Lexi." I say, as I see myself out.

"That may be true." Lexi yells at my back as she watches me leave. "But at least I am not homeless. I tried to warn you. I simply can't handle one more thing."

Hate is the demise of Lexi Kensington. She hates the person she's become but she can't help herself, and I can't blame her.

I knew her for exactly who she is--- and I loved her anyway. I got what I expected. Love let hate win.

CHAPTER ELEVEN: STONED BY THE OG STONER.

Chapter Soundtrack: "Right By You" by John Legend

I need help, but I won't ask for it again. Lexi did me a favor by refusing. She reminded me of my place in this world. I don't belong in upper-middle class suburbia, but I am not poor. I am rich with purpose. There is a reason I am alive and it has little to do with material gain. Money is not my master. I already have everything I will ever need. I am a child of God. I am not forsaken.

Suffering. I am suffering by choice, not by circumstance. I am the reason my life is difficult. I am the reason I have no place to call home. I am responsible for my failures, just as I claim the right to own my successes.

"You've always been jealous of me." My phone buzzes with a text from Lexi. She continues to attack me. "You will never have what I have. I will never be like you. I am not a failure."

I look down at her messages as I drive, taking them in, but not wanting or needing to answer.

She is right. I am jealous of the things she has. I wish I was receiving child support and that my daughter was still with me. I wish I still had my beautiful home and my thriving business. I wish I hadn't allowed myself to fall so low, but I can't undo the consequences of my choices so easily. The road less traveled is my pilgrimage. I needed to lose everything so I could be ready to have everything worthwhile.

"Hello?" My phone buzzes again with another text, but this time it's from Justin. He is home and I am not there. "Your stuff is gone upstairs. Please tell me you didn't do something stupid." He asks.

My first instinct is to react, to reply, but I know my silence will speak more than any words I might muster. I have nothing to say to either one of them, both people are a waste of my energy.

I am tired, too tired to continue driving safely. My windows are rolled down, even though it's cold outside, even though it's raining. I need the elements to keep me from crashing. I can barely keep my eyes open. I am falling asleep at the wheel.

"Dad." I call my father to let him know I am on my way to his house. "I am in trouble." I admit when he answers.

"What's going on?" His voice is gruff. "I am busy over here." He says.

"I need a place to sleep." I say. "I will be there in thirty minutes."

"It's not a good time Amber." My dad does not encourage me to continue. "What's the deal? Did Justin kick you out or something?" He asks, but I won't tell him.

"I am on my way." I say before hanging up on him. I do not allow him the opportunity to reject me further.

There is a reason I do not turn to my parents when I am in trouble. My mom is not capable of helping me and my dad is not willing, or at least that is what I tell myself. The truth lies somewhere in the middle of intention and expectation. I expected my parents to be a certain way, to be a certain kind of people, and when they weren't I decided I could do better on my own, without them. I deserve better than the best they gave me.

Humble. I am grateful for the pain that humbles me.

It's easy for me to admit how callous and disrespectful I've been over the years, but it's difficult for me to write about my family in a way that does not perpetuate the disrespect I am known for. I intend to honor them by sharing this story, but the act of telling it is dishonorable. My father does not want to be written about and if I were a dutiful daughter, I would respect his wishes.

 "My life is not anyone's business." My dad warned me soon after I began writing a blog. "You keep running your mouth on the internet and look what it has cost you. Your writing is hurting people Amber. When are you going to wake up?" He had asked and implored.

I can only hope my parents will find it in their hearts to forgive me for all I've done. I was born to write this book. It is the reason I am here, my purpose fulfilled. I am not writing it for me. I am not writing it for them. I am writing it for the world I will leave behind.

When I die.

I am going to die.

There are four vehicles in the driveway when I arrive at my dad's, but I know he doesn't have company. Two cars are there for parts, to keep the other two hoopties running. Everything my father owns is dilapidated, including the house, which he only rents.

His grass is tall. It looks like it hasn't been mowed in months, but then I am not surprised. My dad has never been one to spend time on upkeep. He does not care if his lawn in manicured. He cares to make sure no one bothers him. KEEP OUT. NO TRESPASSING. There are obvious signs posted, but the aesthetics are even more of a deterrent. His home is unapproachable by design. Curtains closed. Gates locked. GO AWAY. I know he doesn't want me there before I knock. I knock anyway.

My dad opens the door to let me in, but he does not greet me. He leaves that task to his dirty little dog. Scout jumps on me as soon as I enter the house. My dad insists I give his furry friend my full attention. "Say hi." My dad says as he heads back to sit in the kitchen. "He missed you."

"Hi Scout." I say in respect to my dad's request. My acknowledgement is dismissive though. I would prefer to not be bothered. His dog is not important to me at the moment, but admitting it would be unforgivable, so I pretend. "I am happy to see you. I missed you too."

"Give him love." My dad scowls at me from his chair. "He needs pets. Give him some pets." He says.

I don't want to pet his dog. Scout is filthy mop of stink. "It looks like he needs a bath and a haircut." I say to my dad as I indulge him. I pet his dog like I am handling a bag full of rancid trash. My nose is turned up in obvious distaste. I hope my dad doesn't notice, but he does.

"Get down there and give him some love." My dad insists I show even more affection, while I struggle to offer even the slightest bit of care.

"I gave him love." I say, taking a chair in the kitchen. "My allergies are acting up." I use an excuse, but my dad does not buy it.

"I see." He says quietly, through clenched teeth. I can see he is disappointed by my efforts, but I do not have it in me try.

My dad has always been too surly for pets, until the day he was adopted by the neighbor's Yorkie. Buddy. The dog's name was Buddy.

Buddy belonged to a house up the road, but he didn't like where he came from so he ran away as often as he could. Daily. Buddy ran away to visit my dad every day and so often that the family who owned him finally conceded. My dad adopted the dog without intending to, but it was short lived.

Buddy was murdered by a group of teenage boys soon after the family gave him permission to adopt. The boys used the animal for target practice, for sport, for fun. My dad had called me screaming. "They shot my dog Amber. He's dying. He's dying in my arms. I can't save him. Please God. They killed him."

My father howled in visceral anguish as his little Yorkie drowned in its own blood. The bullets punctured his lungs, but did not kill him outright. The animal died slowly, but too quickly for there to be any aid. I sat on the phone with him as he pleaded and wailed, "He's dying Amber." He said it like I should help him, but I didn't know how. "Oh dear God Jesus. They killed him. How could they do such a thing?"

I knew I would lose them both. Buddy had been a joy to my father, happiness previously not permissible. The dog allowed him to be loved, when previously he had been denied and deprived. Undeserving. Buddy was the only good thing in my dad's life, a rare creature comfort in the depravity of his tortured existence. The blood on his hands would steal the light in his soul. The dark would claim him again.

If I let it.

I could not save Buddy from dying, but I could bring my dad back to life. I knew he would never get another dog so I took away his choice. I used all of the money I had to buy him a purebred Yorkie puppy, just nine weeks old. I didn't wait for time to pass, for him to have a chance to heal. I bought his new puppy on the very same day Buddy was murdered and then I drove it up to him in the morning, as a surprise.

"Dad. I need you to come out to my car. I need help carrying something." I called him from his driveway. The tiny puppy had crawled up on my shoulder to nestle under my chin. It was barely bigger than a chipmunk, the nape of my collar was the perfect cradle.

My dad came out of his house looking as dilapidated as the structure. He loomed like a dark cloud with vacant eyes. "What is it?" He asked, without coming closer.

I remained in the driver's seat. My door was open. The puppy hidden in my hair. "I got you something. It's heavy. I need you to come here." I said, motioning with one hand. The puppy squirmed a bit, but remained sleeping in its perch.

My dad lumbered over slowly, only to stop just shy of being reachable. I would need to get out. He wasn't going to come all the way to me. "Close your eyes and hold out your hands." I said, as I swung my legs to exit the vehicle.

My dad did not budge, nor did he give any indication he planned to. He squinted at me as if his eyes had been scorched. "What is that?" He asked. The puppy was awake, unsettled by the turn of my legs.

"Your hair is moving." My dad accused.

I reached up to pull the pup from the tangle of my locks. I placed it in my lap so my dad could get a better look. "It's a puppy." I said.

"I know it's a puppy." My dad grimaced. "Why is it here?" He asked as he moved forward, as he came closer.

"I bought it for you." I said as he reached out and took his pup.

"No." He said, as he pulled the tiny dog up to cradle on his shoulder. "You had no right. You shouldn't have done that." He complained as he patted his puppy like a newborn baby getting a burp. "Hi there." He whispered to the dog as he turned his back to me. "Let's get you inside little one. It's cold out here."

And then he left me without another word. He took his dog and he went.

"Scout is the best gift I have ever been given Amber." My dad continues to press me about his dog. "See him. Get down there and see him." He says, wanting me to get down on his level. Scout is not much more than six pounds full grown. He comes up to my kneecap when he stands on two legs with his front paws up.

"I see him." I say, refusing to indulge. "I need to talk to you."

"What's wrong with you?" My dad asks. "You can't take a minute to be nice. That's really too much?" He chastises me for my selfishness without considering my needs.

I am dilapidated, falling down in front of him, but he refuses to acknowledge I am in need of a brace. He offers no grace as he scrutinizes me.

"I am guessing you finally got the balls to leave that asshole you were living with?" He asks, pushing a pipe across the table. The bowl is loaded with fresh greens.

I take the pipe and enjoy a toke before I reply. The weed is musky and dank. I choke back a cough as I exhale. "Yes." I reply. "I left this afternoon."

"What happened? I thought you were going to tough it out until you could get your shit together financially. What about your business? What are you going to do now?" He unloads his barrage of questions in rapid fire, like I should have it all lined out quickly. Like I should have come to him already prepared.

"I found a letter from Whorie Laurie in his backpack." I start to explain, but he cuts me off.

"So?" He glares at me. "What the fuck does that matter? He's not your boyfriend Amber. He can talk to whoever he damn well pleases and it's not any of your Goddamn business." He barks at me, right and angry.

"That's not the point." I glower back at him. "I wouldn't expect you to understand."

"What don't I understand Amber? That you poked your nose where it didn't belong and then got butt hurt about it? That you moved out and lost your place to run your business? That you don't have anywhere to go and not enough money to make it on. Over Whorie Laurie? You let that bitch win. I thought you were smarter than that." He shakes his head. "Fuck Whorie Laurie. Fuck Justin. When are you going to learn? They never mattered?" He berates me for acting on my emotions.

Smoke. The smoke leaves my mouth in lacy tendrils. It curls around my nose in skunky incense as I relax to the heady high. I am being stoned by the OG stoner. My dad is the father of all philosophy, but he lobs the truth at me as if he's trying to maim me with it. He is right though. I am responsible for my undoing. My choice to leave was impulsive and irrational. Prideful. I allowed myself to be played and to what gain?

"You'll be better off." My dad concedes as I succumb to my own failure. "You should have left that prick a long time ago. He was using you."

"Using me?" I ask, surprised by my dad's assertion. "What was he using me for?"

"Think about it Amber." My dad scoffs, holding the pipe out at me like a tuning rod. "He strung you along to hide the truth of who he really is. You were part of his facade. You were part of his lie. He's gay. Have you forgotten that?" He asks. "He likes to be fucked in the ass by other men, when are you going to get that wrapped around your head. The women he dates are irrelevant. He uses them so he can live his lie in secret."

Justin is a man with secrets. Justin is a man with shame. It's a shame I am one of the few people who know the truth and it's a truth I can't easily tell.

CHAPTER TWELVE: SECRETS AND STRAP-ON TOYS

Chapter Soundtrack: "S&M" By Rhihanna

This book is an ethical dilemma. My blog was plagued by the same challenge. I don't know how to write about the life I have lived through without damaging other people, without exposing secrets that should be kept.

I know better than to out Justin to the public. He has lived his entire life in hiding. Three ex-wives and a son. The people closest to him are clueless, but how could they not know?

> **SUBJECT- I CAN'T KEEP IT TO MYSELF ANYMORE**
>
> *Hey there. Nice ad...gorgeous cock (still drooling). My stats: 5"10', 155, thin, fit, 7" cut. I have a little experience, but want much more. I also crave the feeling of a cock sliding in me, but am versatilely minded and would want to link up with someone who wants to give and receive. Have a live-in girlfriend so discretion is paramount. Here's a few pics...message me back if interested...fuck that*

cock...imagine myself stroking it with lube and climbing on top for a ride.... Can you host tomorrow mid-day? I am in Lacey. Shit! Can you email me back at JustinH420@gmail.com. I did not mean to message you from that other email.

I discovered Justin's secret because I cared to know. I was the live-in girlfriend; the reason discretion was paramount. I moved in with him soon after he professed his love, soon after he gave up Whorie Laurie. His choice to cheat on me was unforgivable, his homosexuality unfathomable. I would have never guessed, and I barely believed it when the truth presented itself.

He's gay?

I wanted someone to tell me I was wrong, that I was making a mistake. I had called Lexi in hysterics. "Help me. Oh God, I need you to help me. I need you to come over right now."

Lexi drove as fast as she could, but it was not fast enough to stop me from losing my shit.

What if he gave me an STD? What if he infected me with HIV?

Justin's sexuality was a death sentence, a deal breaker, the end of all good things. I called my dad as I waited for Lexi to arrive. I was crying so hard he couldn't make out what I was trying to tell him. He answered the phone to my screaming sobs.

"Calm the fuck down." My dad yelled back at me on the other end of the line. "I mean it Amber. Either talk to me like a normal human or call me back."

I forced myself to find some composure so I could share the news. "Justin is gay dad. He's been cheating on me with men on Craigslist. I found emails and pictures. He had plans to meet someone." I managed to inform him before my crying resumed.

"I see." My dad said quietly. "Well, you better pack your things and get the fuck out of there." He suggested I only had one option.

I should have taken my dad's advice. I should have left immediately, but I stayed to reconcile. Justin was my next phone call. I called him while he was still at work even though I knew it was a conversation best had in person.

"You are gay!?" I screamed at Justin as soon as he answered.

"What?" Justin was understandably confused. "No, I am not gay. Who told you that?"

"I found your emails Justin. I saw the pictures." I assaulted him with the facts.

"What emails?" Justin did his best to pretend he didn't know what I was talking about.

"Fuck that cock. Imagine myself stroking it with lube and climbing on top for a ride." I read his email back to him. "Can you host tomorrow mid-day? I am in Lacey." I continued to present the truth. "You've been cheating on me with men. You are GAY." I repeated myself.

"Calm down." Justin remained cool, his voice lowered. "I am not gay. I have not been cheating on you. Listen, I am just about to head into a meeting. We will talk when I get home OK? I love you." He said. "Everything is going to be OK. I promise." He assured me before hanging up. "I have to go. We will talk soon."

Things were not OK when Lexi arrived, nor did they get better when Justin returned home later. His betrayal was too much for me to handle sanely. I was losing my mind at the same time my heart was breaking.

"Are you sure he's gay?" Lexi asked before I sat her down in front of his computer. "Are you sure he's been cheating? Maybe he is just exploring a fantasy? Maybe it's just chatting and nothing more?" She is positive, always positive, even when the worst needs to be reckoned with.

"Read the emails Lexi. You tell me. Is he gay?" I asked her to give me a second opinion, but I knew she would come to the same conclusions. "He was making arrangements to meet up with the guys he's messaging. It doesn't seem like harmless chatting."

Lexi scrolled through Justin's messages with wide open eyes, exhaling deeply before replying. "You are right Amber. I am so, so sorry. Justin *is* gay. What are you going to do now?" She asked me to have answers I was not ready for.

What am I going to do now?

I would have left. I should have left. I didn't though. I stayed to listen instead. I stayed so I could understand what he must be going through. I stayed to assure him of his worth. I stayed so he could know he didn't need to keep lying. His sexuality did not make me love him less. It made me love him more.

Justin came home from work as if nothing had happened. He smiled as he came up the steps. He remained leisurely and chill, stopping to pet the dogs, opening the day's mail. He acted as if it were any ordinary day, while I stood there as if my child had been returned from school dead in a pine box. I was mortified by the found transgression. It was a catastrophic event. He remained unmoved, as if there was nothing significant worth mentioning.

"We need to talk." I said the breakup words.

He wasn't fazed by them. "Yes, I know. We will talk. I am going to have a cup of coffee first and watch a little news." He said, on his way to the kitchen.

I followed him, staring down his back so I could face the front of him. He kept his body turned away from me, his eyes everted. "How was your day?" He asked, as he poured himself a cup of cold stale coffee. The brew was left from the morning. It was long bitter from too much time exposed.

How was my day?

His question and demeanor were infuriating. I wanted to yell, "How the fuck do you think my day was you cheating bastard." Instead, I said nothing. I stood there with a toad prince stuck in my throat, croaking on a wicked spell.

Beep.

Beep.

Beep.

The buttons on the microwave sounded like a bomb about to go off. The microwave hummed, droning warplanes, as it warmed his coffee. I remained mute, holding my fire, but my mind continued to scream at him. "Who the fuck cares about what is happening on the news. Fuck your coffee. Talk to me you asshole. Talk to me."

I wanted him to be immersed in the tragedy of my trauma at the same time I wanted him to be the reason I could be removed from it. Maybe he could explain away all the pain I was feeling and if he couldn't maybe he could at least help ease the suffering. I was a racehorse with a broken leg stuck at the gate. The race was not starting soon enough for a bullet to the face. I needed him to put me down completely, to end it. He needed to watch the news.

Ebola was the headline of the day. An outbreak in Africa was creating world panic.

What if he gave me an STD? What if he infected me with HIV?

Justin sat watching the news in the same fashion he made his coffee. His body remained turned away from me. He slumped to huddle over his cup of java, his eyes were glued to the screen. "Ebola is some scary shit." He mumbled to the room without acknowledging me.

Not as scary as all of the diseases you *may have given me.*

I shivered to think about the health risks. I shuttered at the thought of all the men.

How many men has he let fuck him since we've been together?

It was easy for me to imagine the worst because the worst is exactly what I found. My imagination ran wild with torrid images of hairy legs tangled together in filthy bathroom stalls. Bent over asses, cheeks spread. Spit for lubrication. Tiny fissures, small tears, blood, and cum. All were cracks to let infection in.

I wonder if he lets them cum inside of him.

143

Justin doesn't wear condoms. He doesn't like them. He does nothing to protect himself and yet he's worried about Ebola. The irony jeered at me.

"Can we talk now?" I asked, unwilling and unable to wait further.

Justin turned his body toward me but kept his eyes on the screen. "Football highlights are coming up next. Seahawks." He replied, glancing briefly in my direction before turning all of himself back to the television.

The Seattle Seahawks were in prime position to make it to the Super Bowl that year. The team was on fire, with many speculating they would win the entire thing. I couldn't blame Justin for wanting to follow. On any other day I would have been wrapped up in the 12th man frenzy, anxious and excited, hopeful that this could really be our magical year. Maybe we would win the Super Bowl, but I wouldn't be around to celebrate. If he refused to talk to me, I would leave.

I sat to watch the highlights, but I didn't see them. Justin consumed my pornographic consciousness.

"Fuck that cock. Imagine myself stroking it with lube and climbing on top for a ride."

Justin watched football, while I watched him get fucked. It was sick, but I couldn't turn away from it. He moaned and he wriggled. Gyrating his hips, writhing on a shaft attached to nobody I could determine.

"Touchdown" Justin exclaimed, jumping up from his seat on the couch to cheer for a replay of the game he'd missed. "Yeah baby." He clapped his hands together as I imagined his orgasm. He blew his load while he rode that cock. I heard him moaning in pleasure over the 12th man's roar.

"I am not gay." Justin said finally, and only after the game highlights had finished. "They were just words Amber. Harmless fun. I wasn't going to do anything with anybody. I am not cheating on you." He gave me his explanation like it should be easy to believe, to accept, but there was no way I could let things slide.

"You were making plans to meet the guy you were messaging. You were cheating on me. You can't cheat on me." I asserted my accusation while declaring my expectation moving forward. He had cheated on me. He was not allowed to cheat on me again.

"Do you want to sleep with men or are you craving the stimulation of anal sex?" I asked.

This question caught his attention. He stopped watching the television and turned to me. "What are you asking exactly?" Justin did not answer the question directly. He toyed with it instead. The sparkle in his eyes was playful. He was enjoying himself. "I obviously prefer sleeping with women." He purred.

I wasn't exactly sure why my question was relevant or what I intended to do with his answer. He could have said, "Yes, I want to sleep with men." That answer would have been easy to deal with. I am not a man, therefore I would be unable to fulfill his needs. We would need to be done with each other. We would need to break up.

I wondered though.

I wondered if his cheating was a beast of necessity. I tried to put myself in his shoes. How would I have broached the subject had it been me? "Hey honey, this might seem weird and unusual, but I've really been craving a cock in my ass. Do you think you could help me with that?" The idea was absurd. There is no way I could have had that kind of conversation with him. Maybe he cheated on me because he had to. Maybe he did it to protect and save our relationship. Maybe he assumed I would not be receptive to his needs, that I wouldn't understand them.

I tried to understand where he was coming from, but he gave me very little to work with. "Maybe toys are an option?" I blurted out my suggestion.

Justin started laughing, moving closer. He took my hands in his and kissed them. "Toys?" He teased me. "What exactly do you have in mind? I didn't think you were that kind of girl." He said, bemused. "You want me to purchase a strap-on?"

I smiled meekly, nodding my head. "I think that's exactly what you should do. Maybe you can buy one on Amazon?"

He expedited the shipping. Three days later I became a chick with a dick.

CHAPTER THIRTEEN: FAG HAGS AND DOUCHE BAGS

Chapter Soundtrack: "Crazy Bitch" By Buckcherry

"I must have quite the ego. I believe I can fuck a gay man straight." I laughed at myself before admitting. "I have no idea how it's going to go. I've never done anything like this before."

"Gurrrrlll, you best be ready to work it." Devonte drawled as he sipped his chai latte. "Your man wants the dick. You may have a new sword, but can you slay?"

Devonte is one of a handful of gay men I know. He is not simply out. He is flaming. I called on him for advice and he was loving every minute of it.

"Should I even be doing this?" I asked him to assure me I was making the right choice, but he did not oblige me.

"What do you think is going to happen after you do?" He asked. "If he really is gay there is nothing you can do to change it. It won't matter how good you fuck him. He won't be able to give it up. He will continue to seek out men. Can you live with that?"

"No," I admitted. "But he insists he's not gay. Do the same rules apply if he is bisexual?"

"Bisexual, TRY-sexual." Devonte bent his wrist and flipped his hand down as if to wave off something pesky. "He ain't foolin' anyone but you honey. There are two types of bimen: gays in hiding, and gays in discovery. He may be willing to sleep with you, but if you were really his preference, he wouldn't feel the need to lie and cheat. That was a total douchebag move on his part. What he did is not right, nor is it fair. You deserve better girl."

"So, you don't believe it's possible for him to be bisexual?" I asked.

Devonte shook his head, "Look, my personal beliefs are a bit different than those in my community. I believe sexuality exists on a spectrum. There are not straight people and gay people. Those lines are too severe. We are just people. Sex is different for all of us. Your man needs to start being honest with himself, so he can be forthright with you. It's entirely possible he is not gay, but then how do you explain his affairs? You didn't catch him cheating with women. His choice is telling."

"Do you think this is a phase? Do you think he's just experimenting?" My questions were indicative of my level of denial. I was much like Justin. I refused to acknowledge the truth of his actions.

"Do I look like a mind reader to you?" Devonte flips my question back at me. "I don't know your man and by the sounds of it you don't know him either. How can you be with someone you can't trust? You are sharing your body with a stranger. How good can sex be under those circumstances------regardless of gender preference? His sexuality is not the problem. Your relationship has much bigger issues." He said. He laid it all out to me like he was Dr. Phil, but I felt like I was on an episode of Jerry Springer.

"I am assuming he is a bottom and not a top based on the strap-on he ordered." Devonte continued to try to put the pieces of my puzzle together. "Do you know what kind of guys he's into? Twinks, Otters, or Bears?" He asked me, but I was clueless as to his reference.

"Top or bottom?" I asked, trying to make sense of it all. Is that the way it works when you are gay? You have to choose one or the other? I always assumed gay guys took turns in various positions and what the hell is an Otter?"

"Honey, No." Devonte was amused by how little I knew. His perfectly shaped eyebrows arched higher as he smiled. "I am a top. I will only ever be a top. My ass is an exit only." He said, as he smacked his own behind. "It may be beautiful, but I don't play that way."

"Funny, I always thought all gay guys like anal sex." I admitted. "It never occurred to me that there should be a designation of preference, but that makes sense. Please explain Twinks, Otters, and Bears." I implored him to continue my rainbow education.

"Bears are exactly the way you'd expect them to be. Burly, Brawny, men. Masculine and strong. Think--- flannel, beards, and baseball caps. Bears come in two shapes--- beefy or blubbery. Some are soft and huggable and some are full out meatheads. These are the dudes that watch football and drink beer." Devonte explained.

"I am an Otter." he said. "I am too pretty to be a bear and too manly to be a Twink. You can tell I am an Otter because I have impeccable taste and style. I am runway fierce." He said with glee and glam. "Some of us are more flamboyant than others. Otters can easily be mistaken for straight men if you don't know what you are looking for. We are predominantly masculine, with dashes of the effeminate. Otters are the guy's guy."

"Twinks are fairy princess gays. They love glitter, glam, and drama. These queens are bitchy like yapping Chihuahuas. Probably because they are all hangry. Twinks are typically waif thin. They can be seen eating salads with a girlfriend, or sipping fruity drinks at a club. I call them Peter Pan Pansies because they never seem to hit puberty. They are smooth and hairless, much like Robert Pattinson in the movie Twilight."

"I think Justin must be an Otter." I said, fascinated. "It's a miracle anybody comes out of the closet. Being Gay sounds super complicated. You don't just need to come to terms with your sexuality you also have to choose which category best describes your identity. Do Bears typically date Twinks? Is the masculine always drawn to the feminine?" I asked the last question, but then thought better of it. I knew the answer before Devote elaborated.

"Bears date Bears. Bears date Twinks and Otters. Like I said before, sexuality exists on a spectrum. We are all into different things. What are you doing to protect yourself?" He said and then asked, switching the subject.

"Protect myself?" I asked. His question had caught me off guard. "Honestly, nothing. Justin refuses to wear condoms and I won't make him. I feel like every day is a ticking time bomb. He's going to give me something eventually. I am going need to figure things out or I am going to need to break up with him. My uncle died of AIDS. It was a terrible death. He looked like a skeleton when he passed. He rotted like a tomato gone bad on the vine. He was a living corpse, one of the walking dead, until the disease took his last breath. He died in the early 90's back when HIV was an epidemic in the gay community."

"Gurl, you need to call your doctor TODAY to get on PrEP. What you are talking about is no joke." Devante was reverent to my plight. "I've lost loved ones as well. I get it about the condoms. I don't like wearing them either, but I learned to jimmy up after my third battle with gonorrhea. I thought my shit was going to shrivel up and fall off." He grabbed his crotch as he reminisced. He grimaced as he remembered the pain.

"Your man really is a douchebag. If he cared about you he wouldn't be putting you at risk" He said, leaning into me. "And if you cared about yourself, you wouldn't allow some dickhead to put your life in his hands. You need to take responsibility for your own fate, your own health. You need to make appointment today. You have a daughter to think about, a full life ahead of you. Don't let this dude ruin your future. His path does not need to be yours." My friend implored me to love myself. He said all he could to save me.

"I will call my doctor today." I squeezed his hand as I assured him. "I promise. What is PrEP? You mentioned I should ask my doctor about PrEP? What is that anyway" I asked.

"PrEP is a pill you take daily to avoid contracting the HIV virus. The drug prohibits the infection. We gays eat it like candy. Studies have shown that PrEP reduces the risk of getting HIV from sex by about 99%. The problem is that some people get lazy about taking their daily dose. The medicine only works if you take it consistently. Condoms are still imperative Amber. You need to make him wrap his shit up." Devonte was right about a lot of things. I was lucky to have him as friend.

"So when is he going to harness you up? He asked. "When are you going to try out your new dick?"

"Tonight. It came in the mail this morning." I replied. "I haven't opened the box yet. I figured I'd wait until he gets home."

Devonte smiled, his warm hazelnut eyes were flecked with glimmering gold. "You are about to become a pegging fag hag." He chuckled.

"A fag hag?" I asked. "What is a fag hag?"

"A fag hag is a straight woman who is in love with gay men. You want to be one of us darling, but it's an exclusive club."

CHAPTER FOURTEEN: HOW TO FUCK A BOTTOM OTTER IN HIDING

Chapter Soundtrack: "Paris (Ooh La La)" By Grace Potter & The Nocturnals

The dong is flesh colored, but the harness it attaches to is black. This bothers me. I want it to match. I want it to blend in with my skin, to look like it's a part of me.

I am not sure what I should wear with it. How does one make a strap-on fashionable? Should I bust out my hooker heels and lace myself up into a leather bustier? Should I wear a bra or go topless? Does he want me to be masculine or feminine? It would be easier to plan my wardrobe if I understood my character.

Who will I become when I have my dick on? I most certainly won't be myself. Amber Garibay is not kinky. She barely puts out. If anything, she's asexual, or at least that is who she was when she was married.

I am not the person I used to be and I am not the person I am now.

This much was certain as I stood to examine myself in the full length mirror. I had decided that no clothes would be better. My reflection was naked and exposed.

Full breasts. I am a couple of cup sizes bigger than when we first met. The weight was coming back on slowly. Too many cheat meals. Round hips. I was lean and fit at the beginning of our relationship. Now I am curvy. Not fat. Curvy. Fat would come later, if I continued with my food and wine benders.

The dick was larger than I expected. Justin chose to order the seven-inch dildo. I knew the length was a bit more than average. I was surprised by the girth. "How in the world are you going to fit that in you?" I had gasped when we opened the box together. "There is no way I could take a dick that big." I exclaimed.

Justin was not discouraged. He pulled it from the package to examine it closer. "It's impressive isn't it?" He asked with glimmering eyes. "We have lube."

I tried to put the harness on myself, but I couldn't figure it out. There were too many straps and too many buckles. Justin got on his knees to help me with it. I looked down on him as he tethered me up, my ridged prick poked out near his face. He was in perfect position to give me a blow job--- too bad I wouldn't feel anything if he did.

I would like to know how it feels to get my dick sucked--- if I have a dick--- and I do.

The rod protruded from me like a dead appendage. Massive. It was a bulbous monstrosity. "Gurl, you've got a cock bigger than a black man's dick." I imagined what Devonte would say when I finally showed it to him. "You do know it takes a whole lotta stretchin' to make a hole that big. This is not your man's first rodeo. You've gotta work up to something that size. You'd tear him open otherwise." He would remind me to see the writing on the wall. Justin is not a new gay. He's a bottom otter in hiding.

How do you fuck a bottom otter in hiding?

"You have a new sword. But do you know how to slay?" Devonte's question played out in my mind as I tried to decide how to best approach things. I had never had a dick before. I wasn't exactly sure how to use it.

Maybe I should bend him over and enter doggy-style. It seemed like the easiest position for a first timer. I was worried though. What if I thrust too far in? Was is possible I might actually rupture something internally? What if I accidentally killed him with my giant fake dick? Would I go to prison for manslaughter? What if my strap-on was a deadly weapon? What then?

None of it seemed natural. It was so far out of my universe I transcended. I became.

I didn't want to brutalize him, but I wasn't sure there was any way I could be gentle under the circumstances. I couldn't feel the dick as it was attached to me. It would be difficult to gauge how much pressure I should use.

"How do you want it?" I broached the subject before we began. "I was thinking doggy-style might be the easiest way to start."

He shook his head, motioning for me to join him on the bed. My rubber dick bounced up and down as I walked. It was heavy by at least a pound. I would give him a pound of fake flesh.

He was on his knees when he kissed me. His hand reached out to stroke my cock. I murmured like it felt like something, but there was no sensation. Every part of me was dead in that moment. I was not turned on. I was in my head.

"This is your life now Amber? You are about to fuck a dude in the ass. Is this what you really want?"

The voice within urged me to reconsider what had already begun.

"I want you." I whispered as we kissed. I stroked him as he stroked me. He poured lube over our hands and then he reached back to add some to his ass.

"Abort." My inner voice pleaded. "This is can't be happening."

It was happening though. Justin laid back on the bed with his legs spread wide. "Grab some pillows." He said, as he used one to prop up his pelvis. It took three to get the angle right and then he was prime to be entered.

"I don't want to hurt you." I said, as I grabbed the base of my shaft. I would need to guide it in carefully. I used my hand, so I had some feeling.

"I don't want you to hurt me either." Justin said. "Go slow." He wrapped his legs around me like a grappling spindly spider. Then he pulled me in for a black widow kiss.

The cock did not go in easily, but there wasn't any blood. I was relieved when I didn't kill him and encouraged when I saw his eyes roll back in pleasure.

"Stay there. Stay there." He used his hand to push back on my thighs. He stopped me from going any deeper. "Just give me a minute." He said, catching his breath. "It's a lot to take in."

I almost laughed out loud at his statement. It was a lot to take in. This was by far the craziest thing I had ever done and I knew it was only the beginning of more to come. From prude to crude. I was no longer prim and proper. I was a freak in the sheets. Nasty. It was a nasty affair.

He had me fuck him missionary for a while. Slowly at first, and then with a bit more fervor. I was careful, but also merciless. No longer worried about pain. He deserved what he had coming to him. He asked for it.

"I want to ride you." He said as I was thrusting. "Get on your back.

I obeyed, getting into corpse pose. He climbed on top of me and began to bounce. I felt nothing except for the air leaving my lungs. It was hard to breath under his movement. He was heavy as he impaled himself.

He rode me as if he were unaware of my presence, as if there was no one in the room except his fantasy. He kept his eyes closed. His mouth open. His cum landed on my belly when he finished. I should have been done with him then, but I stayed.

I stayed and he used me like a tool.

I stayed.

He used me like the fool I was.

CHAPTER FIFTEEN: WRONGS WITHOUT RIGHTS

Chapter Soundtrack: "Another Day in Paradise" By Phil Collins

"We are just not working out. You need to see it Amber. We can't keep doing this." Justin Hayward thought he had good reason to break up with me. He sat me down to explain, wise to the certainty he'd settled on. He served it as if it were a saucer of warm milk and I were a kitten happy to be lapping. He wanted me to agree with what he was offering. He wanted me to think he had my best interest at heart, that he was doing me some sort of favor, that it was right to call us quits. "You are the only one that refuses to see we are wrong for each other."

I sat across from him in dumb silence. The rage came quick. It burst from within like a cherry bomb had exploded in the middle of me. My fists flew like shrapnel. I punched him like a man punches another man. With a closed fist and another one coming.

I kicked Justin's ass because he deserved it. Fair retribution. He's lucky I didn't kill him with all the hell he put me through. Whorie Laurie. Men on Craigslist. And now Jenny. Justin loves Jenny.

My dad was right. I should have left him a long time ago and for a moment I allow myself the gleeful pride of knowing I've finally done it. I am free from my twisted hell.

I will not return to Justin's, but I have no place else to go. My dad's place is a temporary reprieve. I cannot stay here.

"You know you can stay here if you need to." My dad offers at the same time I reject the possibility. I watch as Scout stands in the corner, lifts his leg, and pees.

"SCOUT." My dad yells at his animal. "No." He says, too late. "You do not go potty in the house." The dog cowers briefly before scampering over to him, wagging its tail. My dad smiles at him, reaching down to scoop him up. "Your daddy loves you good boy." He praises his dog as he stands to slide the back door open. "You go potty outside." He says as he sets him free. He is gentle. My dad is rarely gentle.

There isn't much carpet free from soil and piss. The shag is crusted over with filth, hard from dirty droppings, mottled dark from spills and dog markings. The odor permeates, an acidic astringent. Pet urine and marijuana smoke. The house is dank and dirty.

"This is his house." My dad reminds me of his dog's importance. "He pisses because I wouldn't let the vet chop off his balls." He says proudly. "I wouldn't let them take his manhood." He loads another bowl as he explains. He acts as if I am not already familiar. "He's my boy."

I scrutinize the condition of my dad's place as I accept his offer to take the first toke of fresh greens. He hands the pipe to me as I look around. The furniture is sparse and mismatched. The couch is a bright orange floral, long tinged

165

brown from time. From the 70's but not wrapped in plastic. The sofa is much like the carpet, soiled and stained. I rarely sit on it when I come to visit. I am afraid the grime will stain me too and besides, I am allergic. Dust and pet dander. The fabric is laden with asthma triggering pathogens.

There is a coffee table directly in front of the couch. It's made of pressed wood, simulated oak. The piece is long dated and out of fashion, not an antique worth collecting, but rather junk typically given away to Goodwill. This particular table would only be worthy of a trip to the dump. There are two glass rectangles that make up the top of it and one of them is broken out and missing. You can't set anything on that portion. Half the table is an empty wood frame with no functional purpose. The other half is piled high with old magazines and random leavings--- a pair of fingernail clippers, a few pill bottles, a bowl full of dust covered rocks.

Dust. There is a thick film over everything residing. The filth is alive and breeding. "Fuck you." My dad yells at his television, which is always on and typically turned to FOX NEWS. "What a bunch of crooks." He shakes his head. "I can't believe what they've done to this country. It's criminal." He laments.

I don't reply to his tirade because I don't have anything to contribute. I quit following politics after I realized my life is too scandalous to be presidential. "Have you been watching this shit?" My dad asks, gesturing toward the two suits talking on his screen. "I've been telling you to pay attention. You better pull your head out of your ass Amber." He warns. "It's a God damned disgrace and if you think you are removed from it you're wrong. They are going to ruin this entire country."

I indulge him by watching. "Bridgegate scandal hits Christie" A headline scrolls lazily along the bottom tickertape as two old men drone on in debate. "Former deputy chief of staff, Bridget Kelly, and Bill Baroni, former deputy executive director, convicted of seven criminal counts -- including conspiracy and fraud."

I am clueless. The named mean nothing to me, their crimes withstanding. The news strikes me the same way the Ebola scare does. I jeer at the irony. My dad frets over the deplorable deterioration of America as his own house falls down around him. He worries about a nation who could care less about his citizen. We are the people--- and he's not one of them.

"I miss my family." I mumble to myself, shutting out the news on the television, returning to the headline of my day. I don't imagine my dad is listening, but he is. He catches my words like he smashes flies, with a slam.

"What in the hell do you mean by that?" He asks. His face is contorted into a mask of scathing disapproval. "What family? Justin and Justice? You better not be talking about them. They were never your family. They were a fantasy you concocted in your head. You destroyed the only family you ever had with that blog of yours. Remember that?" He berates me for my history. "You threw your marriage away so you could run your mouth, so you could write. How does it feel to be left with the nothing I told you would be coming?"

He blames me for this book I am writing and all of the writing that came before it. I know better than to let him dissuade me though. This book is going to save us all. It will help him rest in peace. I pray he never reads it, for fear it will change things.

"Why can't you just support me?" I retort. "Why is it so hard for you to be encouraging?" I ask.

He scoffs, "Snivel, Whine, Whimper. What do you want me to do? Hold your hand, pat your back, and lie to you? I am always encouraging. I encourage you to THINK. I encourage you to be WISE." He says, emphasizing my need for intelligence. "I warned you back then, no one is ever going to pay to read your writing. It's not worth a dime. You had a good thing going with your photography business." He shakes his head. "You should have stuck to that."

I sneer at him, insulted by the wrong he is, bothered by his selective memory. "Do you forget my husband was the one who asked me for a divorce, and he did so BEFORE I started writing my blog, BEFORE I became a writer?" I raise my voice to yell. It feels good to belt it out. "He fell out of love with me because my photography business was all consuming. Do you remember that? My BUSINESS is the reason I no longer have a family dad. NOT MY WRITING." I glare at him.

He glares back, wronged, and insistently right. "Yeah." He concedes. "He should have never done that. Your husband was an idiot, but it's still your fault. You could have saved your marriage. You could have kept your photography business going." He says. He wants me to have all the good things returned as they were, without remembering they were never as good as they seemed.

"I tried to save my marriage dad." I reply. "I shut down my photography business to appease him--- to make my husband happy. I needed a new career as a result. I decided to become a writer. Why is that so impossible for you to understand?" I ask him to see things simply and he does.

"Let me tell you something." He says, leaning in. "One day you are going to need to wake up and face reality. You think you can just waltz right into a new career and you are going to make it, but that's not how things work. Who's going to pay you Amber? Who's going to give a damn?" He asks, implying I was doomed back when I started. "Believe me when I tell you, no one will buy your book. You are wasting your time and talents. You need to put your focus back on what you are good at. You need to continue to rebuild your photography business. It's a shame you don't have a studio now. You keep making it harder on yourself." He reprimands me for choice to leave Justin's in the same way

169

he blames me for my divorce. The right choices remain the wrong ones.

CHAPTER SIXTEEN: DEAD GIRLS ARE VERY SAD ENDINGS

Chapter Soundtrack: "Unwell" By Matchbox 20

What does death sound like? Will my ear freeze to it like a tongue stuck to metal in winter?

My breath is a shallow wheeze. I watch my chest rise and fall, labored. I am struggling to breathe. The attack came the way I expected it would. It came in the darkness while I slept. It waited until I was dreaming --- defenseless--- and then it took my breath away.

Asthma is the reason I am awake at 3AM. I can see the clock through the dim light coming from the kitchen. The lights are still on because my father is still awake. He is a creature of the night, nocturnal. He does not wake to meet the rising sun. He wakes to the schedule of his grow lights. They are set to come on at night.

My dad tends to his marijuana crop while the civilized world sleeps, under shrouds of darkness and nefarious mystery. He watches over his plants like they are little green lambs at risk of slaughter. He stands guard as they take root, branch out, and then bud. He cultivates his treasures until they can be harvested. He loves them like they are all of the stars in the night sky, full of wishes made, ripe with dreams.

My lungs itch. My throat is tight. I am being strangled by invisible hands, squeezed by a demon from the inside out. "You need to get up Amber." The voice within warns me.

"You will suffocate if you allow this to continue. You need to get up and give yourself a treatment before you find yourself back in the hospital."

I choose to ignore the warning. My nebulizer is close by, but I forgo the medicine. I am tired of fighting off the inevitable monster of my demise. "I can't breathe." My mind panics from the deprivation, but I remain unmoved.

I will not get up.

I will not take the medicine.

Not this time.

I give up my life with smug defiance. "You want me? Take me then motherfucker. I am tired of you toying with me." I scream internally as my chest continues its rumbling wheeze. It heaves and sags like a roof about to cave in. I need to cough, but I can't catch enough air to expel anything, so I huff instead, panting in short shallow puffs. "You can't just lay here and die Amber." The voice within insists. "Quit acting like an asshole. Get up and take your medicine. You don't have time to be messing around with this shit. Dead girls don't finish books. Dead girls are very sad endings."

"I want my family back." I whisper as I begin to cry. The tears are hot, while I am cold. "I want my family back." I repeat myself, crying harder. The sobs sound like gasping ghosts--- unnatural, undead. "I want my family back." A raspy voice calls out in the shadows, anguished and empty, torn and forlorn. The plea is coming from my person, but it doesn't sound like me.

"Please Lord," I beg God to hear me. "Please give me my family back. Please God. Please."

The night is filled with unanswered prayers, tears, and the wheezing of my troubled breathing. It sounds like dying sounds. I am frozen by it, stuck, like a tongue melded to metal in winter. I would move away if I could, but my flesh would come off with it. I make myself sleep instead. I drift off to leave the nightmare of my waking hours, hoping my dreams will offer some refuge.

Maybe my prince will find me there.

Maybe I will wake to his kiss.

If I wake up at all.

Maybe I am a dead girl,

Without a happy ending.

CHAPTER SEVENTEEN: LOOKING FOR LOVE IN ALL THE WRONG PEOPLE

Chapter Soundtrack: "My Little Girl." By Tim McGraw

There would be sunshine if it weren't for his curtains. My dad keeps them closed at all times. It's nearly noon, but he's not up yet. His rumbling snore is louder than my nebulizer. My machine hums in cadence with his slumbering. Both are disruptive. I would prefer to sit with my thoughts in silence. I would prefer to be anywhere but here. *Here* is a place I don't belong. I wish I had somewhere else I could go.

"Hi." A single word is sent to me by text. It's from Justin. It's the first I've heard from him since I left.

I stare at my phone, unable to answer. I don't know what to say--- so I say nothing.

"When are you planning on moving out?" He asks, sending me another text. "Your things are still here." He reminds me of what I already know.

I lay there on the soiled couch, still wheezing, inhaling the medicine I should have allowed myself the night before. He has good questions. Maybe he can answer them too. I remain as I was, barely breathing, on the edge of my own life.

"How's Blondie?" He asks about my dog, *our dog*. She was our dog before the unhappy ending. "I stepped in a pile of

Elvis shit this morning." He writes about the other dog, *his* dog. "With bare feet. I nearly slipped and fell in it. I had too much to drink last night. I still have a pounding headache." From dead air to small talk. He blows up my phone with random musings.

It takes me some time to reply. I want to talk to him like nothing's changed, like we are still amicable friends, but I am so far gone I am barely human. Alien. I am trapped on a foreign planet, nothing I knew is familiar anymore, especially not the people.

I lead with an apology. "I am sorry you stepped in shit. That sucks." My reply is short. I don't have anything left to contribute. "I am looking for a place to move to. I will keep you posted." The phone falls from my hands, landing with a thud on my chest. Listless and lethargic. I can't be bothered to try. I've said too much already. I would have preferred to have said nothing at all.

The phone vibrates where it landed, buzzing with a new message. I don't bother to pick it up. The exchange is already too painful, sandpaper scrubbing at an open wound. It doesn't matter what he says to me. He's dead as far as I am concerned. There is no point talking to ghosts from the past. They keep you haunted by it.

What about my future? What kind of life will I make for myself now that I am free from Justin?

I WILL MAKE TEN MILLION DOLLARS WITH A RUBBER CHICKEN

I barely have any money. I don't have a place to live--- but I am wealthy. It's imperative I don't lose myself in tribulations. I know my circumstances are temporary. I believe in my ability. I've been down and out before, nothing ever keeps me there. I am a spider building a web in Tornado Alley. The wind blows away everything I've built, everything I've worked for, but it can't stop me from creating more to destroy. As long as I am still breathing I can create any future I envision.

As long as I am still breathing.

I finish the first treatment, but my breathing is not much improved. A high-pitched wheeze whines and then wanes to a chorus of lower rattling. I sound like an accordion being stepped on, an instrument gasping a garish death tune. The medicine isn't working, but then I am not surprised. The air in the room is noxious, thick and gritty with exasperating particulates. I would find better health sleeping on the streets, but then I would have no place to plug my breathing machine in should another attack hit me.

I would not survive an apocalypse, and yet the end of days are here, for me anyway. There is a happy world outside, teaming with possibility and triumph. I could be a part of it. I could thrive and be prosperous if only I could breathe.

I can't breathe. I am going to die if I stay here.

My will to live supersedes the anguish of my impending doom, but it's not enough to make any of it worth it. I refuse to remain on the losing side of struggle. I've spent my entire life trying to escape where I came from, trying to make something of myself. I've worked too hard to die with nothing. I've worked too hard to die *for* nothing. Asthma will not be the death of me.

Unless it is.

I squeeze a plastic vile of medicine into my machine, another hopeful dose. This treatment will have to work and if it doesn't I will drive myself to the hospital. It's a routine I am long familiar with and one that is completely unnecessary. My asthma can be controlled with the proper medicine, but I cannot afford the steroids that keep me breathing right and my insurance company typically denies the coverage.

The snoring has stopped. My dad is awake in the other room. I wonder what his mood will be as I posture myself to face him. I know he means well. I know he loves me, but his approach is often debilitating. "You need to wake up Amber. Your writing is not worth a dime. No one will buy your book. You are wasting your time." His previous words play over and over in my head, a broken record on a broken road.

The odds have always been against me. I was born holding a losing hand, but what can I do other than play the game as it is. Life is not fair and I won't waste my time wishing that it could be. I will find a way to change the cards I was dealt and I will do so without sacrificing my good soul, without losing my integrity.

"I am not going to love you." My dad warned me long ago. "If you want to act like a little bitch, if you are a cheat, a liar, or a whore. I won't love you. I don't give a shit if you are my daughter, if you are my kid. If you want my love you will earn it by living respectfully."

The love in my life has always been conditional, with one exception. God loves me regardless of sin. God loves me because of my sin. He is the one that allows me any possibility, through him I know everything is possible, including my impossible dreams. I am not a liar, a cheat, or a whore. I could be though. I could be a lot of things, but I have chosen to become a best-selling author. My choice is not disreputable, but my dad would have me believe that it is. "Stick to your photography! Your writing is ruining your business." His urgings linger as echoing doubt. He could be right. This book may very well be the end of my photography business and if it is I will need to adjust accordingly.

"Morning." He greets me shortly, stumbling sleepily ahead to slide the back door open for Scout. "I am sorry about that." He says, eyeing my nebulizer.

I nod at him, shrugging. A misty cloud of vapor floats up from the plastic spout I am sucking on. My disease is not his fault, but I know he blames himself. "Did you make yourself some coffee?" He asks because he knows caffeine helps open up my airways. "There are fresh roasted beans by the microwave. Did you see them?"

I nod again, confirming I was already aware of the coffee, but I am lying. I hadn't bothered with anything in his kitchen. I have been awake for half the day, but I haven't put any effort into it. Taking my medicine is the only exception and the choice was made out of sheer desperation. I could no longer tolerate slow suffocation.

He goes to work on the coffee, pouring beans into the grinder. He takes pride in the brew, the coffee being of the finest quality. "There is fresh cream in the refrigerator." He says. "I purchased it directly from a farm up North. You won't find anything like it in a supermarket. Did you have some?" He asks.

My dad is a man who allows himself few delights, but he revels in most things locally grown and produced. "I also bought sweet cream butter and goat cheese. There is nothing better on earth. I promise you." He says. He's proud of his treasures, wanting to indulge me by sharing.

"I did not see the cream." I admit, telling my first truth of the day. "I'd love to try it though." I say, returning to more fibs. I don't typically like fresh cream in my coffee. I prefer chemically processed powdered creamers. Garbage my father would abhor.

He smiles, tickled to be able to share the experience, to show me something new and special. "I will make you a fresh cup." He insists. "The coffee will do you some good." He says with obvious concern. "It's not helping is it?" He asks about my breathing treatment. He can tell I am still struggling to get my breathing under control.

I shake my head, pulling the mouth piece away so I can talk. "I am on my second treatment now. I took some Benadryl. Nothing is working so far." I admit.

His face contorts with pained expression. "You have no idea how much it hurts me to see you suffer with your breathing." He says, as he pours me a cup. "I wish there was something I could do to help you."

I offer him a feeble smile, hoping to alleviate his worry. "I will be OK dad. I promise." I say, keeping my breathing short and shallow. I don't want him to hear the raping rasp of my strangled lungs. "Justin sent me a text this morning." I change the subject and the focus.

He scoffs, immediately incensed. "Fuck him. I should drive down there and kick his motherfucking teeth in. Let's see what he has to say then." He glares at me as he pours himself some coffee. "What did he want?" He asks.

"He wants to know when I am moving out." I say, flatly. "He wants me to come get my stuff."

"I'll bet he does." My dad's jaw clenches tight like his face which is gaunt with scathing contempt. "I hate that little pansy prick. I'd like to show him what it means to suffer. He's dammed lucky I have some control. It's all I can do to refrain myself." He warns, pacing the kitchen.

I stand to join him, before taking a seat in the dining room. The coffee is helping. I am breathing better than before. "I already kicked his ass—remember?" I remind my dad of my former glory. "It didn't make me feel any better and it certainly didn't teach him any lessons." I say, trying to deescalate the hostility. Justin would not survive my father's beating. My dad would punch him into fleshy pulp and then he'd go to prison for it. "Violence is not the answer." I suggest there is a better way, while wishing for easy redemption.

"I heard you crying last night." My dad says, softening. "It nearly killed me to hear your pain. I feel like a half-lamed cripple. What kind of man allows his only daughter to be maimed? I should have protected you from that monster. I should have gotten you out of there. I feel like I've failed you." He laments, joining me to sit, admitting his own helpless defeat. "It hurts my heart, Amber. I hate knowing how much he's hurt you."

I reach for my dad's hand, giving it a squeeze. "You can't blame him dad. His choices weren't born of malice. He didn't intend to hurt me. He lied to protect me from the truth of who he really is. It can't be easy for him. He's living a lie, skulking about in shadows of deceit. He's never going to be brave enough to come out of the closet. I can only imagine what that must be like. I allowed everything that happened in our relationship. It's my fault, not his. I could have left him. I should have left him. I chose to stay. The pain endured was my choice." I say, taking responsibility for my part in things.

My dad does not allow me to be the martyr. "You are wrong Amber. It's not your fault, not any of it. Yes, you chose to stay, but you made that choice out of love. Justin had choices too. He could have chosen to return the love you gave to him. He was lucky to have you in his life. You are a fine woman. He should have cherished you, but instead he used you and abused you. You were there for him with unwavering faith and adoration. You were willing to accept his kinky perversions, and all you asked was that he be honest, that he be faithful. Now he's moved on to another girl while he takes dick up his ass during his off time." He balks at the absurdity. "Justin never deserved the love you gave him and you most certainly didn't deserve the pain. Just be glad he's not your problem anymore. Jenny can deal with him. They are perfect for each other."

"I wish I could warn her." I say, feeling bad for the both of them.

My dad is quick to stop me. "Why!? That woman doesn't care about you. She only cares about herself, about fulfilling her own selfish desires. She was messaging him while you two were still a couple. I bet she encouraged him to leave you so she could step in. She deserves the pain that's coming. You should let her have it." He says, shaking a finger in my direction. "You have no idea how good things are. You are free to sit back and enjoy the shit show that's coming. Jenny will have it worse than you ever did. Trust me on this."

I sip my coffee quietly, contemplating the future to come. I don't know Jenny, but I feel bad for her. I wish someone had known enough to warn me in the beginning. I am the only one who knows Justin's secrets. I want to pay her the courtesy I was never allowed, but I know she will not be open to receive it. I could tell her the truth, but she'd never believe it. I know the truth, but it hardly seems real. My dad is right. I am best removed from the equation.

"I need to show you something." My dad says, interrupting my line of thought. "You mentioned wanting your family back--- as if you no longer have one." He stands to leave the room, but pauses to say more. "I am your family God dammit. Your daughter is your family." He berates me for the insult of my previous insinuation. "We are the only family you will ever need. You keep looking for love in all the wrong people. I am here for you Amber. I have always been here for you. I am your dad." His eyes are filled with tears, his voice with pleading passion.

"I know." My reply is quiet. I am thinking of a family that's not the same as the one he's offering. A family that includes a husband, a man who will never want to leave me. I am thinking of a home that has a place for me in it, of a lifestyle that is pure and healthy.

"You have no idea how much I've sacrificed." My dad says, as he walks out the door. "You look down on me. You act as if I am below you somehow."

I know he's right. I've always believed myself to be better than where I came from. A pang of guilt and forlorn sadness pulls me off my high horse and into humility. I owe my father more than any credit I've allowed, but still, the family he offers is not enough. It never has been.

"Here." My dad returns to the room, plopping a bag on the table. "I want you to count it." He says, pushing the sack toward me.

Money. There is more money than I can possibly count. I look up at him, my mouth falls open with shock. "Holy shit." I murmur, astounded. "That is a lot of cash."

My dad stares at me intently. "I've always been here for you Amber. You look at my house, at the things I own, and you think I am poor. You think I am a failure. This money is yours if you need it. I've been saving it for you, for your brother. I go without so I can save, because I know you may need my help and I want to be able to provide. You do not need to go back to Justin's. I have enough to help you find a new place to live. I can cover your rent while you rebuild your business, while you rebuild your life."

"How long did it take you to save this much?" I ask in numb disbelief. "There has gotta be at least thirty thousand dollars here." I say, guessing.

"That's fifty grand." He says proudly. "I've been telling you to be smart with your money. This is what I meant. I don't go out to eat. I don't buy myself fancy clothes, or brand new cars, nor do I enjoy vacations. I don't even buy myself chewing gum when I am standing in line at the grocery store. I save." He urges me to grasp the importance of his lesson. "You are not destitute. You are not without hope. I go without to ensure you will be OK. I am your family Amber. I am your dear old dad." He smiles, a kingly smile. Prideful, but without vanity.

"How long?" I ask again about the time.

"Six years." He replies. "It took me six years to squirrel that money away."

"Six years," I repeat his words as if forever has passed and in that moment I realize it has. I have lived my entire life without ever really knowing the miracle of my dad.

CHAPTER EIGHTEEN: RESIDING IN FALSE TRUTH

Chapter Soundtrack: "Baby Girl" By Sugarland

I can't spend my father's money. My situation has changed, and yet it hasn't. I am my father's daughter and so I must share his sacrifice. I must go forward without comfort as he has. I must endure without luxury. Moving into a home rent free is a luxury I cannot afford. I appreciate knowing my father is able to provide a safety net, but I must honor all he's been through to secure the means to provide it. He has gone without and so will I. I will need to find my own way. I will need to make my own money, to secure my own future.

I do not currently have many options. I do not have the means to rent an apartment and even if I did----where would that leave my business? I need a place to run my photography business. I need a studio.

Justin's place was ideal because it offered me the best of both worlds at a price I was able to afford. He lives in a split level home, his bedroom and living space are upstairs. My bedroom and business space are on the floor below. Rent was $500 a month with utilities included.

I could rent a house with my father's help, one with space to live and work from, but doing so would be a mistake. My business is not generating enough revenue to support the cost of renting and I do not have confidence that it will as things stand. $25,000 has been my yearly average for three years running and that's before write-offs and expenses. I am not willing to blow through my father's life savings on a gamble. I need to work with the numbers I have and trust the facts as they are. I do not make enough money. I cannot continue working as a photographer.

"Hey you." I receive a text message from Justin. "I've been looking for a new roommate. Have you had any luck on your end?" He writes to ask if I've made any progress.

"Yes." I reply as if I am able to move forward, but the truth is I am stuck. "I've been looking at houses for rent online. There are not many on the market available in my price range." I admit some part of the truth. I *have* been looking. I can't afford *any* I've found. "I will be driving back to Olympia to look at one later today. Do you mind if I swing by to grab some of my stuff?" I lie to him because I must. He will pray upon any weakness I expose. I need to proceed from a position of strength.

"Cool." His reply is short, but open. "Yeah, that will be fine."

My dad comes in to check on me. He's been out in his grow room for most of the afternoon. "Well?" He asks about my house hunting.

I can't tell him there aren't any options so I tell another lie. "I found one that may work. It has three bedrooms and a garage big enough to convert into a studio space. I could find a roommate to help cover the cost." I offer a solution, even though I know it's not really feasible. "It even has a fenced yard for Blondie." I say, turning the computer toward him so he can get a better view of the listing I am looking at.

He smiles, "Rent is only $1,700. If you get a roommate in there you won't be paying much more than you were at Justin's." He says. "I would call on it. Don't worry about the money. I've got you covered."

His offer is not one I can accept, but I call on the house anyway. A man named Brett answers my inquiry. He indicates the home is still available to rent, so I book an appointment to go see it. "Yes. I can be there by 2pm today." I confirm my availability. "I will be on my way shortly. The drive is a bit more than an hour."

My car does not start easily. The key turns over in the ignition, but the engine does not fire up. It sputters briefly and then dies. I crank it again, giving it some gas. Vroom. My Mustang catches and sparks to life, just barely. "Come on girl." I talk to my vehicle as if it will help. "I need you to run for me. Please don't leave me stranded." I implore. The car shudders and shakes, but keeps running.

It's difficult to keep my composure with so many things going wrong. Nearly everything I own is in disrepair. My car and my camera being the most impactful. I know it's only a matter of time before both of them will need to be replaced. I have nothing saved to ensure I will be able to do so when the time comes and its imperative I remain debt free.

Stress. My stomach is twisted into a knotted ball of sickening stress. The back of my head throbs with a pounding ache. I've barely eaten these past days, which is fine by me. I have weight I need to lose anyway. I am fat, unhappy, and broke. There is some comfort in knowing at least one problem may be easily rectified. It won't take me long to lose the extra pounds at the rate I'm going. I don't mind that I am starving. I only wish I could think straight.

My thoughts are clouded with the despair of overwhelming problems. The solution being money I do not have. I will apply for jobs, but after fifteen years of self-employment there is little I qualify for above entry level and at what cost? I should be able to land something for minimum wage, but a job like that will eat up all of my hours and still leave me impoverished. I remember how it feels to work for hours on end and still not make enough to keep a roof over my head. I started my business because of that struggle. I am not willing to go backwards, but I may need to for awhile. Some money is better than no money and besides, I will need proof of income if I intend to secure a place to live. Landlords are funny that way. They want to make sure their tenants can afford to pay.

I can't afford to pay for the house I am considering renting, but I go through the motions as if all is well. I even allow myself false hope. A feint "maybe."

Maybe, I can let me dad help me? Maybe, I will have a new home by the end of this day? Maybe, everything will work out.

Maybe, I have the wrong address?

I arrive to the address on the listing, but the house is not right. I am in a new build development. 1629 Brentwood Drive belongs to a home that will never be lived in. A model home, for new home *buyers* to preview. Before they *BUY.*

I am not here to buy anything. I am not even sold on renting. *"This can't be the place?"* I mutter to myself as I kill the engine. I scan my phone to double check. 1629 Brentwood Drive. The address listed on the online rental advertisement matches the one I am at. There is no mistake of destination. There is something wrong though. The house pictured online is nothing like the house in front of me. They are completely different structures.

I exit my vehicle slowly, wary of a threat I've yet to identify. WELCOME HOME. A spindly sign is staked by the entrance. A lanky lie. I am not home. I have no home. This one holds little promise.

The front door is slightly ajar. I am not sure if I should enter or knock so I do neither. I stand there like a dumbfounded dumbass, duped on the stoop. I've been lied to. I know the truth before I realize the deception. There never was a house for rent. I was lured here by false pretense. But why?

"Amber?" His voice is the only thing I recognize. The door opens to the man I spoke with on the phone. "Brett." He extends his hand to shake, but I do not take to it. He flashes a smile with too many teeth. His grin is carnivorous. "Come in! Come in!" He says, motioning me in with the hand I refused to shake. "How was your drive?"

My drive was fucked because my car is fucked. I spare him the truth of any detail. "It was fine." I reply, curtly.

Brett pretends not to notice me cutting him off. "Wonderful!" He exclaims. "It is a wonderful day for a drive and on such a fortunate occasion! Are you ready to get the ball rolling on your new home?"

"Sure." My reply is tentative. My tone is salty. "Is the house in the listing still available to rent?"

Brett does not flounder. He pounces. "Please, have a seat." He insists. "May I offer you anything to drink? Coffee, Tea?" He caters to my creature comfort like a farmer fattening a pig for slaughter.

"I am fine, thank-you." I say, taking my seat, but only the edge of it. I sit like I am readying myself to leave.

Brett seems to not notice my posturing, but I am well-aware of his. He is primed to his script. He has answers ready for every question I will ask, with good reasons for persuasion. I did not come here wanting to buy my own home, but he will make sure I leave that way.

"I know you have your heart set on renting." He begins. "The answer is yes, we do still have a few rentals available. They just might not be in the area you were hoping for. What if I told you that you could purchase a brand new home for the same amount you were planning on paying for rent? Would that be something you would be interested in?" He asks without waiting for an answer. "You could be investing in real estate instead of throwing your money away each month on rent."

"I do not want to buy a house. Debt is rarely a good investment." I scowl at him as I stand. He is a snake, but I am the one full of venom. "Are you really trying to fuck with me right now? Do I look like a dumb bitch or did you just mistake me for one?" I hiss as I strike.

Brett recoils, "Excuse me?"

"I just drove over an hour because you told me there was a three-bedroom house for rent at this address. Now I am here, standing in a house that is not available to rent, listening to a liar try to convince me I should enter a legally binding financial contract with him. I must be a dumb bitch, or you are a damned fool? Do you have any rentals in Olympia or not?"

"No." Brett admits, finally subdued. "Our closest rental is in Auburn."

I'm out.

Middle fingers UP.

I just came from Auburn.

This shit show is a waste of time.

Time is money and I'm broke.

#howtomaketenmilliondollarswitharubberchicken

BONUS CHAPTERS

Does it matter how we fell in love,

if our relationship ended in heartbreak?

The guy I am dating will have a real name in my novel after I decide whether he's fact or fiction.

Do we have something real and valuable? Or is he a character in a story that will soon end?

CHAPTER ONE: WHO IS JUSTIN HAYWARD

Chapter Soundtrack: "Chances" By Five for Fighting

JULY 9, 2013 THE DAY OF OUR FIRST DATE

"You picked that restaurant to go to? BORING!" Heather was immediately turned off by my choice of first date venues. "These are your memories Amber Garibay. They matter, make them special. You're treating this date like a whatever, but what if it's not. What if he is the guy? What if he matters, and even if you come to find out that he doesn't matter, you do. This is your time, make it count. You deserve to experience something far better than some generic restaurant chain. Text him right now and tell him you've decided to go somewhere else and try these on."

The shoes were adorned with earth-colored beads, a mosaic to nestle a latte-colored stone swirled with cream placed center. The leather was painted red, cut to open toe, and bound to wedges. The wedge itself was the color of hemp twine. I wasn't sure about any of it: shoes, dress, or place to date, but I complied with my friend.

My friend Heather is mostly right and this day she was spot on. The shoes were a perfect complement to the dress she had chosen for me. "You should wear a dress," she said, handing me a pile to choose from. "Guys like legs." The first of her choices was the one I was standing in, already right. It was the color of wheat and sun-softened sand. The hem fell almost too high above the knee, saved to grace by lace, two inches. The stitching was delicate, lending a whimsy of

201

seduction by invitation to examine the craft and detail of thread. It was a wonder to unravel.

"Wear that on your date." Heather told me what to do.

"Where are you going to tell him you want to go?" Heather insisted I tell my date what to do. She handed me a black satin blouse next. It was printed with little brown owls all in wise spectacle. "You should get this too." She insisted.

The shirt I placed in the keep pile without question, but her question went unanswered because I didn't know where I should ask my date to take me.

I stood there in the dressing room like a princess without a fairytale. "Honestly Heather, I thought Red Robin was a fine choice. The last fancy dinner date I went on didn't end well. The guy invited me out somewhere expensive, somewhere I could not afford. He intended to pay for dinner until he realized our first date was not going to include sex with him and other people. He actually had the nards to broach the topic before the main course was served." I explained. "He let me know he wanted to have sex with me, but it would interest him more if I could be open to group sex."

"That guy was a douche." Heather was again scouring the store for new treasure. "How did he react to your rejection?'

"He had a physical tantrum and then an emotional tirade. He thought I was judging him." I answered her, while I examined myself in the mirror. I looked beautiful in my new dress.

"Weren't you judging him?" Heather was fast to the point.

"Yes, I was judging him. I don't want a guy who wants to share me with his friends. I'm looking to meet the man I will marry. There was no judgement beyond that."

"It could have been fun." Heather teased.

"I'm sure it would have been. The guy was hot and really tall, almost too tall. 6'4 or close to it. He looked like the actor who played The Mummy." I tried to explain his depiction.

"Brendan Fraser... No... That's not right. Arnold Vosloo." Heather was quick. I was surprised she could recite the actor's name because I would have been at a loss, but I knew she was right upon hearing it.

"Yes! He looked like Arnold Vosloo, but better looking." I exclaimed. "It really is a shame he had no finesse. I told him he should have worked on trying to seal the deal for himself before worrying about his friends. Maybe he could have turned me." I said, laughing.

Heather was not buying it. "Yeah right. Well, at least you had a nice dinner, and it was memorable, which brings me back to my point Garibay. Imagine a dinner like that with the right guy. You can't meet Justin at Red Robin, Amber. It will sound tacky when you tell your grandkids the story of how you met."

I raised an eyebrow at her, "Our grandkids? You crack me up. I'm not that old and maybe he's going to be another 'NO'. Does the place matter or does the person matter?"

Heather was intolerant and insistent. "Both. Pick somewhere you can sit outside by the water."

I could see her mind Rolodex Oly venues while the scene for my summer romance was set.

"Hearthfire," she said. "You should have him take you there, and wear this necklace. This matters. You matter. You don't know what the chances are."

CHAPTER TWO: A CHEETAH FOR A GAZELLE

Chapter Soundtrack: "Maneater" By Daryl Hall & John Oates

"Unlike other big cats, cheetahs cannot roar. However, they can purr on both inhale and exhale, like domestic cats." –Fun Facts About Cheetahs

I wasn't thinking about Justin or our date as I drove to the restaurant. I was thinking of all the dates I had been on before, some of them perfect, none of them right. "It will take a special guy Amber." My friends took care with their assurances, none promising. "Maybe you are just too picky."

Of course, I am picky. I should be picky.

What kind of man do I want? The internet offered a plethora of options. Online dating was a hundred or more messages a day with most sorts except well-written or well-mannered. One guy wrote to me about my profession:

> *"I've been reluctant to message you since it seems you're a traveling photographer. Not a steady relationship building profession. You're very attractive but I have roots for my 3 girls until they say they are ready to bloom and move on. What is your actual profession?"*

I read his message and laughed out loud without needing to reply. He wouldn't have liked what I would have said anyway. It would have read something much like this. "Dear sir, I am actually a gold digger. I am looking for an old-fashioned man who will take care of me and love me forever and ever. I want to be the number one woman in his life. His pretty, pretty, princess. Will you be my forever friend? Do I look like I need more mouths to feed? Do you really think you can afford me?"

Mean. Single life had hardened me, but then I never wanted to be single. The divorce happened quickly, seventeen years of life and an identity. Amber Garibay. Who was I before the end of myself? What was my actual profession?

I was an award-winning professional photographer and graphic designer before the divorce. I did well for myself too. I worked day in and day out, but I managed to help my husband secure a better life for us. We worked together as a team, me: as an entrepreneur, him: with the steady state job.

Our careers were a perfect complement to each other. Mine was risk and his was the safety net. There was no way we could fail. We were the couple who were going to make the distance. Soulmates. Best friends.

What the fuck happened?

"I am not in love with you anymore." My husband was the first to say it, but he was not the only one who felt that way. I was not in love with me either. I was over-worked. I was over-extended. I was tired of being tired--- and then tired some more.

I was giving all I had and there was nothing left. My best was suddenly barely any effort at all. I had come to a place where I didn't really want any of it. I did not want to be a wife. I did not want to run a business. I could not be a friend. I was barely there to be a mother and yet I was in the same room as my family. Where did my family go?

Letting go seemed to be the right thing to do. It was a loving act to let go of anybody needing to love me in return.

Love is selfless. Our divorce was meant to be a kindness, yet I was left with the obscene. There was no reward for my choice. Karma did not pay me any favors.

Online dating was obscene. It was like playing Russian Roulette with stranger danger. I was always one date away from meeting Mr. Right or one date away from being chopped up and mutilated by Mr. Wrong.

This date felt different though. A Cheetah for a Gazelle. I do not know why I felt safe going on a date with a man who mentioned being a predator looking for prey as his dating profile tagline. I suppose he seemed honest. His profile was creative and refreshing.

He wrote:

> *"Here's some about me, what I'm into and what I'm looking for.*
>
> *I like the sights, sounds and smells of the outdoors and have enjoyed quite a few hiking, rock scrambling, mountain climbing,*

snowshoeing and camping adventures. Don't always start out as adventures, but something always happens. Like being chased by mountain goats, running into a bear and being bit by rattlesnake. Well....the rattlesnake incident was in college and alcohol was involved, but it occurred outdoors and was an adventure so it stays in the profile.

Sorry.

Kind of went off on a tangent there.

Back to it.

Anyway, I'm not always so hardcore when I'm outdoors. A long walk on the beach is nice or just chilling at a local park sippin' on a coffee.

A road-trip in the Jeep, top off and tunes on is always a good time. Doesn't matter where we're going. It'll be fun and memorable. Sound good? We might get along. If two wheels is your thing, got you covered there too.

I'm very fit and do a mix of weights, Insanity, heavy bag work and running. Now that it looks like summer's finally here, I'll be out running quite a bit and would love to have a running partner. Laps around Capital Lake is a favorite - just came back from there. While

I do work out a lot, I'm not some bulky steroid guy, but am well-toned. If bulky steroid guy is a lion, I'm the cheetah. Guess you'd be the gazelle in my wild kingdom. Could be a fun chase. Someone I'd be interested in has some kind of fitness routine (preferable including running)...doesn't have to be too hardcore, but something you do regularly that makes you sweat and keeps you in shape.

I do like my downtime though. When the rain's coming down, a cuddle with my woman on the couch is a good time. Get a fire going. Put in a movie. Ahhhhh.

I have strong creative/artistic urges and have dabbled quite a bit, but haven't yet found one to stick and keep my interest. Blame it on my ADD. Just kidding, I don't have ADD. Crap I need to go buy dog food. Anyway, someone I would be into would have a creative/artistic side whether it's focused on music, art, writing or whatever. Being around people like that is inspiring and motivating. You don't have to be awesome, just into it.

I like all types of food and will try just about anything once. I eat healthy mostly, but love me some pizza (Old School, Dirty Daves, Farellis are a couple local favorites). I like to hit up Osaka for some sushi, washing it down with hot sake...mmm...warms the belly. Like to cook and BBQ and eat dinner on the back deck in the evening with tiki torches all around and pretend I'm in Hawaii. If you like to cook, bonus points for you. Maybe you could teach me some things and it would be fun doing it together.

I'm into music and mainly a rock guy. A few of my favorite (current) bands: Soundgarden, Foo Fighters, Shinedown and Three Days Grace. Right now into the song "Sail" by Awolnation, such a groovy, sexy beat. I do appreciate quality music in other genres too, definitely not a music snob.

My sense of humor is kind of deadpan, sometimes juvenile and sometimes dirty. You've already had a little taste of that I think. I like a woman that has a good sense of humor and can be goofy and dorky sometimes. If you make me laugh a lot, you've won half the battle. I don't expect you to have me pissing my pants on the first date though - so no pressure.

I'm a deep thinker and philosophize at times. If a little MJ is involved I can sometimes unravel the mysteries of the universe (which are forgotten by the next day).

Oh...I'm a huge 'Hawks fan from way, way back...like the beginning. Going to be a fun season. If you're a 12th man too, bonus points.

Not a dealbreaker though.

Gonna wrap this up, finally, with some more about the person I'm looking for...

She's in the local area or vicinity, preferably. The closer the better, but if I think you are that awesome, a greater distance matters less. She has a nice smile and beautiful eyes. She's has a positive outlook on life and doesn't quit when things get tough, 'cause they will. She's funny and has a goofy side. She makes fitness a big high priority in her life. She's adventurous. She has a creative/artistic side. She's cute and kinda short. How short? I'd say shorter than me, but taller than a hobbit standing on a pony keg. She's got an upbeat personality and a good heart."

It seemed like a perfect match on paper. He was exactly the kind of guy I was looking for, even though I was not exactly sure what he looked like or if we would have chemistry.

There were photos on his dating profile, but none that showed him clearly. He was a mystery beyond the mindset he had created online via his writing. It was his writing I was attracted to. I wondered how I would feel about the man in person.

I was thinking about that mystery when I finally arrived to meet my fate, to meet my date. What were the chances this guy would be the right guy?

Maybe my friend Heather knew something I did not. Maybe Justin would be the man of my dreams. Maybe our first date would be the start of something more meaningful than good-bye.

CHAPTER THREE: WHAT'S NOT ON THE MENU AT THE HEARTHFIRE GRILL

Chapter Soundtrack: "Hot Summer Night" By Grace Potter and The Nocturnals

I scanned the parking lot without hoping to find what I was looking for. Justin's jeep was silver. Suddenly, I had an aversion to the color in the same way a werewolf hopes to avoid a bullet made of the same substance.

My heart was a drum inside my chest beating the courage out of me. I wasn't ready for reality yet. I wanted to stay in the moment I was in, which was hopeful. Everything about this day felt right. Heather was right to suggest we move our date to the Hearthfire Grill, which looked like a beach front paradise perched on the pilings of Budd Inlet.

It was the perfect day to sit outside on the patio with the water and the waves of Puget Sound. By perfect, I mean it wasn't raining and it wasn't cold. July might be predictably hot in other regions of the country. The Pacific Northwest is not one of those places. Here, we expect the rain, even in the midst of summer. And yet, the sun was shining beyond and despite the expected.

What did I expect? The question was suddenly there, just as the answer followed like a gnat nagging to race a fruit fly. Both were the same bug.

Expectation was the splatted insects on my windshield. I dared not feel much for them or anything else that is likely to die. Love especially.

Did I expect this date to lead to love? That depended on lust I decided. I am not easily turned on. Chemistry for me is a periodic table of elements beyond any controlled formula.

I surprise myself to reject most everyone as "No. I am not interested." Though, there have been a few I allowed for the sake of experimentation.

Would I? Could I? Feel something again?

I was interested to know if any prince could break my spell. Dating had been less than enchanting, and yet I still believed in fairytales as I parked my car to wait and see about another maybe.

Maybe this guy would be different. Maybe he won't even show up. Maybe was the question in my mouth as I puckered my lips to apply gloss to them. Lip gloss is a sticky kiss, but then what kind of decent woman kisses on the first date?

I was tired of being decent, but then I had little choice in the matter. I had yet to meet a man I could entertain a fantasy with, let alone a real physical connection. My level of frustration had me wearing black leather and dominatrix stiletto spikes.

Someone would need to pay for making me wait so long to be touched. I would take it out on his hide with a whip and hot candle wax. I would make him wear a blindfold so he had no idea what was coming next. What was coming next?

Silver and Black. I spotted the jeep in my rear-view mirror at the same time I took in my reflection. My hair was down and layered to fall just below my shoulders. I had curled it, but then loosened the tendrils to soft waves, which were the color of honey-wheat with golden highlights.

The gloss on my lips glistened as I practiced my smile in the mirror above my dash. Fake. I could not find a genuine smile in the day's collection of grins. The man driving the jeep was a stranger. He was not yet a reason for joy.

He was a poignantly handsome stranger. My eyes locked onto his frame. Justin was lean, angular, and wearing a black tank. He had parked some distance away, so I squinted to see him further.

His body was hard to miss, even though he had not yet existed his vehicle. I was pleasantly surprised by the preview and now even more anxious. My hands were shaking as I picked up my phone from the passenger seat. It was vibrating with a new text from Justin.

"I think I see you." He sent me a message to let me know he had found me.

"Yes. I think I see you too. Hi." I replied. I included a smiley face emoji.

I tried to appear confident, but I felt meager. I was awkward like a girl who had been chosen to be prom queen despite the fact she is an unpopular nerd.

"Justin" I whispered his name to myself as a reminder in case I forgot. I worried that I might. My mind was nearly blank with nervous panic. I had become the gazelle he had written about.

Dinner. I felt like dinner, like a snowy throated damsel about to be drained by Count Dracula himself.

I was in a trance as I pushed the door of my red 97' Mustang closed with the swing of my hip and a bump from my rump.

My car is a beast of heavy metal hair-band nostalgia. It doesn't fit my personality and yet it does. I was in my early twenties back when my car was popular. I had big hair back then, held high with plenty of Aqua Net aerosol hairspray.

My gas guzzling, ozone depleting, American Mustang is the modern doppelganger of me wearing fur to a PETA fundraiser. I rocked it like I had swagger in a song written by Spose. "I'm Awesome."

My date was gorgeous and adorably approachable. "Hi. I am Justin." He introduced himself as if I didn't know who he was.

He reached to take the sunglasses from his face at the same time he motioned to extend his hand for a shake. The glasses he perched like a crown in his hair, revealing smoky grey-blue eyes with flecks of green and hazel. His hair was dark but had gone silver as time had distinguished him.

His smile was easy and inviting, casual, much too casual for a formal handshake. I ignored his hand and reached for a small hug instead. He was taller than me. I curled to stand on my tip toes as he accepted my more familiar introduction.

"Yes. I had a feeling you must be Justin." I teased, still close from our brief hug and even more exhilarated. "You may not have guessed, but my name is Amber." I smiled playfully, as I backed up to take in more of what he looked like up close.

His eyes had my attention again. They were sparkling mischievously at me, the lines laughing.

"Cool." He said casually, playing into my teasing. "I am glad you're Amber. I was kind of confused as to why this strange chick is hugging me."

"Are you complaining?" I asked, raising an eyebrow and feigned alarm. I pretended I was hurt but he was quick to rescue me.

"Complaining? Yes, actually. I think I might have been complaining." He admitted, as he pulled on a button up shirt over his tank. It was the color of smoke to match his steel grey. "I thought the hug should have lasted longer and included more exploring with the hands. I will let you practice after dinner." He laughed easily, extending an arm for me to hold as he took his lead.

Justin was clearly in charge of the moment, which was fine by me. I had been hoping to find a man who would challenge me to want to try.

I found myself wanting to try to master the hug he had just described in a most devouring way.

Hungry. My stomach grumbled to protest not being fed. Taking my time to explore his embrace was an appetizing prospect, but first we needed to master our first dinner together. Except, dinner was not really what I wanted anymore. The meal I was craving was not one I could find on any menu.

CHAPTER FOUR: THE SEDUCTION OF SISTER SARA

Chapter Soundtrack: "Papa Don't Preach" By Madonna

The hostess was young, pretty, and chatty. She had violet eyes and raven colored hair, which she wore down and wavy. Her cheeks were dimpled, and her nose was dotted with Punky Brewster freckles. She might have looked like a proper church girl, had it not been for the curves busting out of her pencil skirt and the cleavage that swallowed her top.

My smile cooled to hear her voice, which droned with too many questions.

"Yes. We want to sit outside by the water. Please take us there quietly. I do not want to hear your voice lady. I want to hear his." My thoughts were tart, but I meant no offense.

She was a vision, but Justin had his eyes on me. I wasn't sure how I felt about it. His attention made me uncomfortable.

Maybe he is undressing me with his eyes.

Maybe I want him to.

"She's my sister." Justin voice broke through my torrid imaginings. He was talking to the hostess about me. He was lying to her. "I just flew in from South Africa." His voice was the sound I had been hoping to hear, but the words he chose made me cringe.

His sister? Did he just call me his sister?

Justin winked at me. I blinked back at him in horror but managed to keep my composure. He was speaking to the violet eyed trinket in an accent that sounded English. I chimed in with the same accent.

"Yes, I missed you terribly darling brutha." I leaned in to snuggle close to his arm, resting my head affectionately on his shoulder. He smelled as good as he looked. The cologne he was wearing was light with subtle nuances of woody citrus and pine.

The hostess was impressed with Justin much like a college coed with a crush on her professor. I watched her posture change as she realized our relationship is not one she needs to be threatened by.

Her breath caught, "Wow. South Africa. That's really cool. I would love to go there." Her voice was husky. She lowered her lashes demurely, hiding her eyes but inviting seduction.

Justin was clearly amused by the spectacle of our darling hostess just as I was glad to at last be at our table and free of the charade. She sat us with a pause that made me wonder if she was going to hand my date her phone number, but her hesitation was short lived and lack luster. "Your server will be with you shortly. Enjoy your dinner." She departed ambiguously.

"Your sister?" I teased him just as soon as the hostess was gone. "Dating your sister is an incestuous choice. Unless of course you were trying to imply I am a nun?"

Justin offered me a devilish grin and beguiling eyes, both of which had me pinned. His gaze was disorienting. His voice toyed with me, low and lazy, like a lion trying to purr with game in its mouth. "A nun? If you were a nun, you'd be the one in 'Two Mules for Sister Sara' and I would be wondering if you had ever been with a man and when I would be your first."

My heart quickened to know his reference. "Oh really? Clint Eastwood style? That is a rather forward way to speak to a sister of any persuasion, don't you think? Maybe I should slap you like they do in old movies? That is a great movie by the way. One of my favorites." I said, flashing him my first genuine smile.

"You know the movie?" Justin seemed caught off guard for the first time, which was fine by me. It felt good to be on top, straddling the conversation. "You did not take me as the kind of girl who watched westerns." He looked pleasantly surprised.

I smiled easily and with fond memories. "I owe that thanks to my grandfather. He seldom left his recliner, and his television was usually turned to AMC. If it's an American movie classic I have likely seen it, though I must warn you I am not one of those super cool chicks who can recite movie quotes off the top of her head."

Justin pretended to be disappointed at the same time he worked to impress me. "All the women I've ever met were natural-born liars, but I never knew about nuns till now." He held my gaze in challenge, which I met like a pawn taking down the king for a checkmate.

"I remember that line from the movie. I'm catching what you are throwing down." My eyes twinkled as our conversation sparked new connections through relatable history.

"You're quick. I am going to need to stay on my toes to keep up with you." I teased, as I sparkled. It was refreshing to find myself in tune with his station. Talking to him was easy, light, and familiar.

He was relatable in a way I had not yet found. I felt myself hoping things would always be comfortable. Being near him was like wearing an oversized sweater darned with cotton fluff. I felt cozy and warm beside him, despite the breeze coming in from the bay. The sun was still shining, but the wind had a bit of a bite to it.

Justin took notice of the wind. "Maybe I should have brought a jacket. Are you cold?" His voiced concern warmed me, but my body gave me away. The hairs on my arms were on end, waving to acknowledge the fact that despite the heady effects of our alluring and budding romance and the bright summer sun, it was cold.

I lied and pretended, "No. I am not cold at all. It really is a beautiful day. I am glad the sun came out for our date. I was afraid we were going to get rained out of our water view. It's nice to sit outside." I said. The wind challenged my lie with a gust that caught my breath and blew my napkin from the table.

Justin saved it from blowing away at the same time he offered me an out. "Just let me know if the wind gets to be too much for you. I want to make sure you are warm enough." He reached over to squeeze my hand. I felt my face flush.

I was warm enough, but it had nothing to do with the temperature outside. I wasn't expecting the reaction to my date to be so physical. My body's response felt like a betrayal to the rational part of my brain. The part of me that insisted I remain in control of both my senses and my ability to make responsible choices.

I wasn't looking for a hook-up and yet there was some part of me that felt I needed one. I ignored it, much like the wind which was now blowing relentlessly. "So, you have a son?" I changed the subject and my attention.

"Yes," Justin smiled proudly. "I have a son. Justice. He's eight. And you have a daughter?"

"Yes," My smiled matched his. "My daughter was born on my 25th birthday. Sapphire is twelve now. I can't believe how fast the time has flown."

"Your daughter was born on your birthday?" Justin smiled even bigger than before. "No way! My son was born on my birthday too. Best birthday gift I have ever received."

"Really?" I was intrigued by the parallel. "That's crazy. What month were you born?" I asked, wanting to know his sign, as if the universe was somehow in alignment with our meeting.

"September." Justin offered easily. "You?"

"January." I replied, "Capricorn and Virgo. I wonder if our signs are compatible." I said the second part out loud and regrettably. Astrology makes me feel like a schoolgirl trying on last names. It was juvenile to mention.

"You are into astrology?" Justin asked, without any indication of judgement.

I grinned sheepishly. "No, not really. I only ever really pay attention to it when I am single. It's silly really. I will actually Google a guy's sign to see if we are a compatible match and if we aren't I will not agree to a date."

Justin laughed. "So, you must have already done your homework because here we are. Tell me. Are we compatible Amber? I have a feeling the stars are on our side." He purred.

I would have answered, but fate interrupted in the form of our waiter who was ready to take our order. "Have you folks decided on dinner or do you still need more time?"

"More time!" My mind belted. "Yes. I can be ready." I said instead. "I am not especially hungry. I think I am just going to stick to an appetizer and drinks if that's OK?" My reply was directed to both the waiter and my date.

Justin closed his menu and handed it to the server. "I was thinking the same thing. The seared beef tenderloin strips are perfect for me and the lady will have?" He put the ball back in my court, but I did not run with it.

"Actually, that's exactly what I planned to order. Let's just stick with that and do you mind moving us to a table inside?" I turned my attention to the waiter, then shrugged my shoulders at Justin in defeat. "The wind won the battle after all. I really am a baby when it comes to the cold."

Justin looked relieved, already standing to switch locations, as the server took my menu and grabbed our drinks to move us indoors. "I will let you in on a secret. I was hoping you wanted to go inside. I am freezing. I am not good with the cold either." He admitted, rubbing his biceps and shoulders for friction heat.

I laughed readily, feeling guilty because I had not read his signs. "You could have just told me you were cold." I said.

"Oh yeah?" His deep voice asked from somewhere behind me. I had gotten ahead of him on the way to the table and now he was taunting my backside. A shiver of delight streaked up my spine as the low murmur of him stuck a chord by invitation. "And what if I had told you I was cold? Would you have come closer to keep me warm?" He asked, pulling me near him without needing to be physical.

"Maybe I would have," I drawled sweetly, sliding into a booth just inside the restaurant. It was easy to be coy with him. My date had potential, but it was still too early to tell. "It's a good thing our server rescued us to move you inside. I might have let you freeze to death instead." I cracked the whip on maybe and let it be a challenge.

It wasn't difficult though. Dinner with Justin was easy like spending a lazy Sunday on the couch with your best friend, a pair of pajamas pants, a mug of coffee, and a favorite movie. He fit the part perfectly, until I felt like he had always been there and always would be.

It was easy to forget he was a stranger. It was easy to forget time. It was easy to forget my own place and I knew I surely had when our server came back to let us know, "The restaurant is about to close. You are welcome to stay a little longer, but do you mind if I go ahead and close out your check?"

Just like that our first date was over. "Wow. Have we really been here that long?" I asked, near shock. "I can't believe we closed down the restaurant. The sun was still shining when we arrived for dinner. It still feels early."

"The night is still young." Justin restored my Cinderella slipper. "Unless of course you have somewhere else you would rather be? We can go for a drive?" He raised his eyebrow with his invitation.

Justin leaned closer. His eyes were piercing, holding me down and captive, until I found myself sitting there without any clothes: vulnerable, exposed, and liking it.

 He handed the server our payment and ticket to leave. "Keep the change." He said to him and then back to me, "You didn't answer me. Is there somewhere else you would rather be?" He asked, with a devilish grin.

"Don't be stupid Amber. You do not know this guy. Play it safe." My conscience implored me to be reasonable, while my body begged me to give it more of what I was feeling.

I wanted just a taste more. "Yes." My mouth moved before any more reason could object. "Let's go for a drive dear brutha." I switched back to the fantasy of my English accent as I stood on weakened legs to meet my end and inevitable corruption.

"A drive sounds innocent enough. Especially when it's with your sister." I said, smiling up at him sweetly.

Justin stood up and close. "You are not like any sister I have ever known, and I never promised it would be innocent." He warned me again, but I could not be careful.

Sister Sara I was not. I was a sinner without want for saving and he was fast like a cheetah cat fixated on his meal and prize capture. Our first dinner was just an appetizer. I left the restaurant wondering if I was always meant to be the main course. Justin devoured me with his eyes, and I knew he did not intend to be left hungry.

CHAPTER FIVE: COPS AND STOLEN KISSES

Chapter Soundtrack: "Wicked Game" By Chris Isaak

Stars. We stepped out into an unexpected twilight. Gone was the sun and the blue of the sky. There was no waterfront. There was no beach. There was no summer day romance. Everything looked like spilled ink: too dark and difficult to read, save for the stars that were flickering like a thousand tiny fireflies.

Buzzed and euphoric I opened my arms to twirl. "The stars are out!" I exclaimed, as I opened my mouth to laugh and breathe in the glory of the night.

"It's rare to see the stars out in the city. They usually can't compete with all of the lights made by man and modern society." I explained my joy, while looking up, mouth still open to drink in the wonder of the perfectly revealed cosmos. "I can even see the big dipper."

Justin was still standing under the halo glow of the restaurant awning, whereas I had managed to spin myself to the center of the parking lot. We were worlds apart in demeanor, which was not surprising to me.

He was cool, collected, and poised--- much like I would expect a man to be. Yet, when I made my way back to him I swore he looked to be on the verge of dancing and spinning himself.

There was an amused energy about his person which only charged my spirit further. I resisted the urge to grab his hand to pull him into the street to dance with me.

Instead, I twirled one last time, but this time not quite so gracefully. I nearly tripped over the tall heel of my wedges, stumbling only briefly before Justin reached out to grab my arm in support. "Hey now. Be careful there." He pretended to scold me for being careless, but his smile was endearing. "You are going to break an ankle in those shoes."

He held out his arm as an anchor and lead. I moved closer still, taking hold of his strength and composure until I regained both my level bearing and my head. How easily I had been caught up in the magic of our first evening. Would there be a second? I found myself asking the question while wondering about what would be next.

Next, was the two of us making our way to his jeep. He opened the door for me before closing me into his ride. I felt much like I did the first time I was tall enough to ride the Zipper at the country fair.

I climbed into the seat feeling like I was grown-up and ready, only to rescind my courage and regain my youthful innocence upon realizing the permanence of my choice. Once we got started there was no turning back.

I was sure I was not ready for what would be coming. I was also sure I wanted it to happen. I had been waiting a long time to be "tall enough" for this ride.

"Where are we going?" I asked, breathless because I had been holding mine.

"I'm not sure." He replied, as the streetlights zipped by us over head. "Do you have somewhere you want to go?"

"Just drive," I replied from the vantage of my seat which was open to the night and the sky. Justin had taken the top off his jeep, which was brave considering the fickle weather.

I liked him more for not worrying about the rain, but then I liked him plenty already and too quickly. I felt like I was sitting in the eye of a storm.

Calm. I was no longer nervous to be alone with him, nor did I care about the destination of our drive. I already knew what was going to happen.

I would not allow myself to be swept away and so there was little more to expect than what was already transpiring. The night was passing by too swiftly and without the danger of any regrettably consequence.

I was in control, grounded like a tree with roots the size of other trees until the fantasy of my desire was destroyed by reason. There was a reason I was here, and it was not to get laid.

I was disappointed in myself for deciding I would not use Justin for sex. I wanted him and the want was uncomfortable. Restraint was the discipline of denying myself much needed pleasure and yet I knew that sleeping with Justin would not allow me any real gratification.

I wanted to give a damn again. I wanted him to mean more to me than a plaything or toy, to be more than a tool for my shallow amusement. I wanted him to entice me with some reason to care.

Justin had one hand on the wheel and another on the radio. He turned the music up to a beat that was hypnotizing and when he did, I sailed worlds away to float outside of myself as the rhythm of a heart still capable of feeling. Electric. My pulse raced as the rush filled my veins with song.

"This is how I show my love. I made it in my mind because. I blame it on my ADD baby. This is how an angel dies. I blame it on my own sick pride. Blame it on my ADD baby."

The lyrics of the song were a Harpy's cry warning of rocks and imminent peril. Would he have a short attention span?

There it was again. That small part of me that was already beginning to care. Would this be my first and last night with Justin and if it was the last, could I forgive myself for not claiming his body as a trophy consolation prize?

His body was enticing like the devil whispering in my ear with a pointed tongue. I was longing for rapture and his physique looked to at least hold the promise of it. How would his arms feel around my body? Or my legs feel wrapped around his waist?

It was the wicked who whispered, but I ignored them. Mostly.

Justin's voice helped break me free of temptation and yet he presented a new one with an offering. "Would you care to enjoy a toke?" He asked, as he opened a small compartment to reveal a pipe already loaded with a big, fat, green, bowl.

"You smoke weed?" I asked, grinning and grateful. "Nice!"

Justin winked at me, turning off the road and into a parking lot with only two lights overhead. The jeep came to stop under the shadows of one of them, allowing us more light than darkness without the glare of any obvious spotlight.

 He turned down the music and opened the sounds of the night before us. Crickets and frogs were the melody as the river rushed nearby. He handed me the pipe. I brought it to my nose to enjoy before I lit.

The bud was subtle and earthy with sweet overtones, "It reminds me of Purple Kush." I described the familiarity, taking the lighter and then a hit.

"God's Gift is the name of the strain. Granddaddy Purple and OG Kush are the parents, much like Purple Kush, minus the color of the bud. Can you taste the grape and citrus?" Justin knew his weed.

I let the smoke out of my lungs slowly. Nodding, I handed him back the pipe. "Oh yeah. It tastes as good as it smells. Thank you." Gratitude was the best expression of the high I felt. "God's gift. Yes, exactly right." I relaxed to the happy mellow of the Indica, stretching out like a cat rolled in nip to purr.

Justin's eyes were on me again. I couldn't look away, or at least that was the compulsion that allowed me permission to stare back, and I was.

I was staring into deep blue oceans, swimming naked on sandy beaches.

"You look really pretty right now." Justin's compliment was a capsizing wave drowning me further.

"Oh yeah?" I questioned his praise while knowing he meant it. I thought to repay the favor with a compliment of my own for him, but decided not to bait his ego. He was already too sure of himself.

He was sure he would kiss me. I could see it by the way he eyed my mouth with probing and curious inflection. What would his lips taste like? Would they be sweet, citrusy, and intoxicating like God's Gift?

There were so many things I wanted to know about Justin. When, for example. When was he going to try and kiss me?

Two lights encroached, headlights, with colored ones on top. Cops? The moment made me a fugitive, guilty as charged. There was no way we would be able to explain away the cloud of Maryjane smoke that had us both hot boxed and high.

Marijuana was newly legal in the state, but we were in a vehicle conspicuously parked in the half shadows of a historical park owned by the city. If the police were here to pat us down the results would not be favorable. My stomach dropped, heart pounding out of my chest. I whispered as if my lowered voice would make our lone parked jeep any less obvious. "Please tell me that's not a cop?"

Justin looked back over his shoulder briefly before turning back to me with urgency. "I think it's a cop. He'll think we pulled over to make out. Now kiss me."

And just like that Justin lowered his head and claimed my mouth with his. The kiss was sooner than I was ready for and not at all what I expected. I hadn't expected to be ramming a frantic and petrified tongue down his throat, nor could I have ever imagined myself actually sucking off his face like a Hoover vacuum and yet that was exactly what was happening.

I was not kissing him with passion. I was kissing him in fear of being caught and taken to jail. I wasn't breathing or making out well. My face was glued to him like a sloppy succubus, until I could not help but laugh inside of his mouth.

The entire scene was hysterical like an episode of "I Love Lucy." I snorted, choking on the obscene humor of it all, pulling away from him to wipe his face off and mine.

"That kiss was close to the worst kiss I have had or given." I laughed openly, both elated and embarrassed to have nearly licked my poor date to death. "Please tell me the cop is gone."

Justin sat back in his seat--- relaxed, lanky, and already recovered from the smattering of tongue I had only recently lashed him with. He smiled coyly, bemused at my dishevelment. "Do you mean that cop over there?" He nodded in the direction of a vehicle that had come to park in the same lot.

It wasn't a cop at all. It was a Pinto. The driver was a slovenly fat man with a scraggly beard and coke bottle glasses. I could see him clearly by the overhead light turned on in the cab of his car. He looked like a pedophile.

"I do not know what is scarier." I said. I was nearly giddy with amusement. "The guy sitting in that car over there, or the thought of us getting arrested for smoking weed."

Justin used his thumb to wipe the side of my mouth before cupping my chin in his hand. "I think that first kiss was the scariest. Let's try it again." He murmured.

He leaned in slowly this time, deliberately. This kiss was not like the first. It was stunning, stirring me into a tea leaf paradox.

I was no longer plastered to the edge of myself, spinning centrifuge. This kiss struck me to the center of my being, pulling me down and into the depths of it.

I might have drowned in his kiss had it not been for the rain. The first drop hit me in the face, wet and full. There was not a cloud in the night sky, but the rain had come. It was the end of our perfect evening.

CHAPTER SIX: RED FLAGS ARE REALITY WITHOUT ROMANCE

Chapter Soundtrack: "Don't" By Ed Sheeran

I did not know if I would see Justin again, nor did I dare entertain the idea of it. We had chemistry, but then "yes" can easily turn to "no." I was sitting on the fence of a double-edged sword nearly cut in two. Should I bother to care even a little?

"This matters. YOU matter. You don't know what the chances are." Heather's previous urging resonated.

If I wanted a second chance at love, I would need to open myself up to at least giving a shit. What had men become to me besides expendable?

They were like clothes you try on in a dressing room with mirrors that make you appear wider than you really are. Grotesque. Dating was a fun house of clowns. "You are not IT. Bring me Stephen King."

Stephen King is not much of a looker, but at least he knows how to tell a story in the way life really is: full of gore and terrible things---- things that will eat you after they rape you.

Dating was not fun for me. There was no romance, only love lost. Desperately seeking. Love lost.

Justin was still too close to his lost love. I knew we couldn't have a chance as a couple after our first date, even though the stars were shining favorably. The night was dark and full of terror flagged red. He was a red blanket in front of a bull. I would be a fool to stand in front of him as a contender. He would surely run me over with blind stupid rebound reaction.

He wasn't even divorced yet. His beautiful bride left him not soon after the alter. His marriage lasted nine months giving birth to no glory except the end of all the love they had created. Love he surely believed in.

What do I believe in? I tried to process the question separate from my thoughts of him but found them intertwined. I believed he must be devastated beyond any soothing or repair, a living corpse riddled with emotional shrapnel. Divorce is not something anyone can survive. I believe in pain and ending. I believe in death. What about love?

I toyed with the possibility in the same way a grieving widow clings to her dead husband's coffin. Maybe if I held on tight enough the dead could regain living. Maybe if I held on tight enough love would remind me that it doesn't die. Maybe I would have held on, but I couldn't.

It was too hot and too blinding. Love was like being lost in the scorch of a desert. All I could see was sand and an hourglass. Only time could tell.

"Hi Cutie. What are you up to?" My phone buzzed with a text from Justin like an alarm set to serendipity. His message was a fortune to rescue me from my thoughts which were muddled with distraction.

"I am trying to study for my test." I admitted freely without wanting to sound like he had somehow been a disruption. "I am glad to hear from you." I sent my text with a smiley face emoji and heart to soften any misconceptions. My experience being that text messages are often misconstrued.

"Your test?" Justin inquired because I hadn't mentioned it previously. "What are you studying for?"

"I have a job lined up as a personal trainer, but I need another certification to qualify." I explained briefly before asking. "What are you up to?"

"I just finished watching Survivor and now I am about to rack out. I was thinking of you though so I thought I should say hello. Do you like comedy?" He asked me if I appreciate humor at the very same time I was humored.

He was watching Survivor and here I thought the show had been canceled years ago. "I've got tickets to go see Jim Gaffigan in Seattle Saturday night. You should come with me." He sent the invitation for our second date before I even had time to process the first part of his message with a cheeky reply.

"This Saturday?" I sent the text thinking of my test and the classes that would come before. It was a two-day seminar with testing at the end of each lecture. I needed to be back in Seattle early Sunday, up at the butt crack of dawn, in order to make the hour drive before traffic turned it into a three-hour drive.

I also needed to pass the test I was driving up there to take. My employment depended on it. I needed the money more than I needed a laugh. I needed the money more than I needed a chance at love.

"Yes, this Saturday. The show starts at nine." Justin confirmed my fear. The show was late and on the same weekend as my test. "We can leave early and have dinner before?"

Temptation dangled more than a carrot at me. Saying "Yes" would be irresponsible. There would not be enough hours of sleep to start the new day fresh and I needed to be rested to keep my sharp mind. Besides, I had not studied enough and still needed to cram.

The date was a bad idea. I needed to decline the invitation.

"Yes. I would love to go. I will already be in Seattle on Saturday attending a conference. You can meet me up there." I went against better judgement by accepting.

"Sweet. I will text you tomorrow and we will line up plans. Going to rack out now." Justin's said.

His goodnight text left me to be wondering about my new life and our second date. He was cute in the same way novelties are bought and sold.

Once upon a time, I was a Beanie Baby collector and the owner of a Rare Princess Diana Beanie Baby Bear 1997 Retired. I spent nearly my whole two-week paycheck, $450, to buy said bear

*because someday it would be worth
more than what I paid for it.*

*I kept it in a glass case, one with a light,
the kind mother might use to display her
crystal collection or grandmother's fine
china.*

*Then, years later, I sold the same bear
for a quarter at my estate sale to a kid
dribbling ice-cream.*

*DIVORCE. "Please come buy everything I
spent my whole life working to
accumulate for less that it is worth."*

*Today the Rare Princess Diana Beanie
Baby Bear 1997 Retired is available to
purchase on Etsy. It can be yours for
$100,000, the estimated value.*

Justin would only be valuable if he stuck around and I wasn't sure I would let him.

I need to focus on my career. I need to create a new life for myself. I have a plan with deadlines looming. I have a plan that includes a rubber chicken and ten million dollars. I have a plan that includes my own suicide. Justin wouldn't want any part of that, so I painted all of the roses red and put my thoughts of him to bed.

WHO IS JUSTIN HAYWARD?

He is not the love of my life.

He is a gay man who cheats on unsuspecting women.

He is fiction.

He is a lie.

PART TWO

BRODIE LOVES AMBER

CHAPTER ONE: FUCKED UP FUCKERY

Chapter Soundtrack: "Irrational Anthem" By Plain White T's

If you read my first book you may have finished it and thought, "What in the hell did I just read? She never did tell us how to make ten million dollars with a rubber chicken."

Forgive me, I really do intend to teach you about wealth building.

Wax on. Wax off.

I invite you to smoke a bowl and chill. Wealth building is a marathon not a sprint. You are going to need to give me some time. If you read my first book you know I had my hands full of fuckery.

FUCKERY

Fuh-Ker-Ry

Noun.

Insidious deceit, treachery, and falsifications.

1) **Pertains to a person, situation, or place that is ridiculous or nonsensical.**
2) **An alternative to the word "bullshit"**
3) **Injustice**

Fuckery comes in many forms and manifestations. My fuckery looks like my boyfriend getting fucked in the ass by men on Craigslist and me being too broke to move out and move on. My first book was filled with fucked up fuckery.

My hands were full.

If you want to make ten million dollars with a rubber chicken you should know...

It's going to be VERY difficult.

(especially if your hands are full of fuckery)

But...

It is possible.

I can prove it.

THIS STORY IS CONTINUED IN MY NEXT BOOK:

JOURNALING AT THE DEVIL'S HOUR:

How to turn $10 into $10 million

4/20/2021